SWING TRADING WITH OPTIONS

7-DAY CRASH COURSE FOR BEGINNERS

STRATEGIES TO MAXIMIZE SHORT-TERM TRADING

MARK STOCK

Table of Contents

Introduction

We've all heard those stories about people who got into trading and instantly made millions. You know, the ones where a person spend his whole day looking at the charts, making moves and walking away with a satisfied smile on his face. What the stories don't tell you is how that same person also probably lost millions. With investment always comes risks and the more capital you risk, the more losses you risk. Luckily, swing trading can help you avoid this problem.

Swing trading doesn't involve millions of dollars. It's not high stakes. It's more like a medium risk/reward type of trading. You'll use the small swings within a market to get a little gain and you won't have to worry about massive losses. Swing trading is the perfect middle ground in trading, offers you the most flexibility and results in fewer risks than other types of trading.

Swing trading is a great opportunity for beginner traders. It results in small gains but also less risk than day trading. It also provides you immediate feedback on your trades, unlike long-term investments. If you want to see results quickly without the risks of day trading, then swing trading is the place to be. This book will help you start your swing trading journey. We'll cover a lot of the why's, what's, and how's of swing trading. We'll even cover how to get the most out of your swing trades.

We'll go over some of the different types of trading and of course, the basics of swing trading. This book will go further into discussing the different types of assets you can trade, and it will focus on trading options in particular. We'll also cover risk management strategies before getting into the how's of swing trading. In that section, we'll look at how to put everything into practice, have some examples of profitable trades, and explain the importance of analysis. By the end of this book, you'll be set up to start your swing trading journey with our seven key strategies for making the most out of your swing trades. If you're ready to start the next branch in your financial journey, keep on reading!

Chapter One: An Introduction to Swing Trading

Swing trading typically involves buying an asset and holding on to it for a very short time. Usually, within a couple of days or weeks, the share or option is sold and the swing trader moves on to the next possibility.

The goal of swing trading is similar to the goals of any investor: to make a gain. However, in swing trading, the gains tend to be smaller than investments where a share is bought and sold years down the road. So why swing trade if the gains are smaller? Because with smaller gains come smaller losses. In this chapter, we will explore the differences between swing trading and other types of trading. We'll also cover some of the basics of swing trading and why it is a good choice for investors.

Swing Trading Vs Other Trading Styles

Day Trading

Day trading is a very active form of trading. It requires minute by minute updates, dedication and a lot of focus. It's not well suited for beginner traders because day traders must have a lot of knowledge and experience in the market. Day trading is also quite risky. Since traders hold on to the asset only for a few seconds, minutes, or hours, they don't get many chances to make sure their asset will provide them with a profit. They can't check the background of a company, the quality of the stock, or the truth about any rumors. They can simply rely on watching their screen to mark changes. The slightest rumor can change their fortunes.

Day trading is like having to cross a seven-lane highway. There are cars zipping by at incredible speeds. On your end of the highway, you only have a small amount of money, but for every lane you can get past, your money will drastically increase. You only have a small window of time to analyze the situation before making your move. Once you're crossing the highway, you might have time to stop before moving to the next lane, but you might not. You have to maintain ultimate focus as you cross or you might miss your next opportunity. Or get hit by a car, which, I don't need to tell you, means serious loss. This is day trading. You have to make fast choices that can result in big rewards or big losses.

If you have a lot of knowledge about the markets, the stocks you're choosing, the economy, etc. then the risk might be worth it. But for many of us, the risks aren't. Day trading is much closer to gambling than investing.

In a five-year study conducted by researchers in Taiwan, they found that nearly 20% of all trade was conducted by day traders. Many day traders can earn a substantial profit, but rarely if ever cover the transaction costs associated. In fact, the study found out that 8 out of 10-day traders lost significant amounts of money, while the other 2 out of 10 make and kept making profits (Barber et al., 2004). So, day trading is not the best option for making and keeping profits.

Long-Term Investments

Long-term investing is, perhaps, the complete opposite of day trading. If day trading is the equivalent of crossing a seven-lane highway, then long-term investment is the equivalent of taking a walk in a park and for every half mile you make some money. It's not a gamble. It's a well thought out plan put in place to get you from point A to point B with slow and steady gains.

Long-term investing can be active or passive, but many people stick with a more passive approach. This type of investing is what most people think of when they learn about investing in stocks. This is the type of investing that our parents and grandparents did. In long-term investing, a person or company takes the time to learn about the asset they're buying. They consider the business aspects of the asset, and consider whether it will stay strong or quickly fade. Then, they buy a share of a company and hold onto it, no matter what. Their hope is that years later, when they're ready to sell their assets, they'll make a large profit. Long-term investors are so sure of their prospects that the slightest dip in the market does not faze them. Even if the market goes into a serious plunge, long-term investors may come out with little damage. Long-term investing can give great rewards, but like any investment strategy, there is always risk involved.

Imagine investing a thousand dollars in a company. The company gets better and your stock values soar. However, maybe something shocking happens to the company or the market, perhaps another recession or the company turns out to be entirely false (hello Theranos). Your stock values can drop like a stone long before you get the chance to sell. Therefore, your once big gains are now a massive loss. As a long-term investor, you'll probably choose to stay with the market and you might be able to make some profit. But you also might not.

Swing Trading

Swing trading is a happy medium between those two. Trades occur over the course of a couple of days or a couple of months. Swing traders use the "swing" in an asset to buy and sell. For example: if you look at a typical stock chart of a company with an upward trend, you'll see a mountain-like graph. There are points of upward movement and downward ones. Swing trading takes advantage of those short upward and downward movements where they can make a potential profit.

Swing trading is a good choice for new and advanced investors because it gives you feedback on a regular basis. Within a few days of starting, you know exactly what happened to your assets, what you gained or lost, and why. It can give you the motivation to continue, because it deals in small amounts of money, losses can be minimized with the right techniques. Swing trading also positions a beginner to learn how investments in the market move before jumping into larger trades.

It avoids the issues inherent in both day trading and long-term investing. Swing trading isn't a gamble on the same level as day trading. It uses smaller increments of funds, relies heavily on market analysis and because the assets are held for some time, there is a good chance that you'll be able to withdraw before the market shifts. It's a slower trading style and the returns may be a bit slower than the possible highs of day-trading, but your returns will be more consistent and it's unlikely you'll gamble away all of your account funds on swing trading.

In swing trading, you'll also get some immediate returns and feedbacks, unlike long-term investing. Swing trading means that you may not make the profits a long-term investor will, but you'll have a closer eye on the market and be able to make a quick profit without risking too much loss. It's the perfect type of trading for a beginner trader, who is looking for some excitement, or a more active role in their trading.

Types of Analysis used in Swing Trading

Swing trading relies heavily on analysis. The whole goal of trading is to make a profit. In swing trading, that profit is small so the risks are small too. You must analyze the risks and rewards of a trade before buying an asset, otherwise you will simply be blindly gambling away your money. When evaluating the risks and rewards, you want to look for entry and exit points and for areas where you want to have a stop-loss. We'll talk more about stop-losses later, but for now, let's look at the entry and exit points.

Swing trading is about small rewards with minimal risks. If you buy a share for $5, then you want to sell it at a higher price, maybe $7. This is a good risk/reward balance. When you reach your $7, that's when you would exit the swing. You want to avoid losing money, which may happen if you hold on to the stock for too long. Clearly, you don't want to sell the asset at the same price, $5, or less. In order to find the best entry and exit points for an asset, you need to analyze the trends of the stock. In swing trading, there are generally two types of analysis used: technical analysis and fundamental analysis. Market psychology can also play a role in understanding swing trading.

Technical Analysis

Technical analysis is the primary type of analysis that a swing trader will use to make their trades. It is based entirely on math and the history of the trend. It doesn't take into account the company, the rumors, or any outside influences. It simply looks at the math and how the stock did in the past to determine the future of the stock. For swing trading, this is often used because assets are not held for a long period of time, therefore many traders don't believe they need to know the history of the company, it's leadership structure, etc. because they won't be holding onto the stock for very long.

For a quick history lesson, you should know that the modern take on technical analysis is the brainchild of Charles Dow.

When using technical analysis, you should keep in mind some of its tenants:

1. All relevant information is already noted in the stock price. This means that you don't have to do further research. All of that information has already been accounted for in the price of the stock itself. Even when new pieces of information come in, or rumors start, these are also immediately reflected in the stock prices. This tenant saves the trader time and they can quickly determine whether this stock or asset is the right one for them.

2. Most of the time, prices will follow a trend. A trend is how the stock prices are doing and whether they are headed in a positive or negative direction. Most stocks don't stay at a consistent area, they have highs and lows, but they often head in one direction. So, if the trend is positive, it's most likely that it will remain positive. When using technical analysis, you should trade by following the trend.

3. History tends to repeat itself. This isn't just an adage about never forgetting the lessons learned from the past. In the market, prices tend to follow the same patterns

over and over again. You can look at charts from 100 years ago and see the same patterns repeated today. History in the market does repeat itself, just like it does in many other aspects of our lives. You can use that repetition to help analyze your asset choice.

So, technical analysis basically focuses on repeated patterns to help determine the future of trends and the value of the stock. Traders will look for specific patterns, or have a set technique they follow in technical analysis to choose their entry and exit points. Since technical analysis is speculation, it's not an exact science, despite having a name that screams "science". It's more of elaborate, educated guessing, and sometimes it doesn't work. This is where bringing in another type of analysis can help you make your trading decisions.

Fundamental Analysis

Fundamental analysis is what you might consider to be the "traditional" kind of analysis. When we think about stock investing throughout history, it involves a long-dedicated time to analyze companies, their leadership, their goals, products etc. All of this gives an indication of where a company's stock might end up. This is fundamental analysis. If technical analysis is driving a ready-made car off the lot without checking its specs, fundamental analysis is taking the time to look at each individual part of the car and car industry before driving it. They are on opposite ends of the spectrum, but both of them can help you analyze a stock to invest in.

Fundamental analysis looks at the intrinsic value of a stock or asset. It checks if everything behind a stock matches its current value or whether the stock is under- or over-valued. This knowledge can help a trader know at what price they want to purchase a stock and at what point do they want to sell. To analyze a stock, analysts often start with the macro and ending to the micro factors. They start with the overall economic environment, move to the industry outlook and finally look at the company itself. There, they will analyze the company's performance and possible future revenue. Using all of these factors, they will establish the intrinsic value of the stock.

If the current stock is undervalued (the current stock price is less than the intrinsic value) then traders will buy that stock. If it is overvalued, traders should not buy that stock. Fundamental analysis is just another way to determine whether a stock's price is worth it or not. It's less about predicting future moves and more about looking at the current status. Fundamental analysis is so detailed that it should and does have several books dedicated to its study. Let's leave it at this: Swing traders often use both technical analysis and fundamental analysis when choosing a stock, they would like to buy into. These two analyses help them choose their entry and exit points to gain the most profit they can.

These two types of analysis can make the market seem so easy to understand. However, they are far more detailed than this little description has given. You should do your research on how to conduct analysis before jumping into trading.

Behavioral Economics

One of the common criticisms of technical and fundamental analysis is that many people believe the stock market can't be predicted. A lot of the times, the stock market is just going to do what it does and technical and fundamental analysis are more like self-fulfilling prophecies than actual predictive outcomes. Some people argue that the markets can't be easily predicted. However, one thing that can be easily predicted is people. And surprisingly, or perhaps unsurprisingly, our behavior and psychology can greatly influence the markets. If you know how to read people's behavioral patterns, it can give you an edge up in predicting your entry and exit points for swing trading.

As humans, we tend to want to minimize losses as much as possible and always hope that there will be a rebound in some way. In investing, this plays out as people holding onto a stock with the hopes that it will increase again. However, it may not and this can lead to some serious losses.

Another aspect of our behavior that can affect the markets is FOMO: fear of missing out. Despite the fact that we all feel like individuals, we're really a herd. And just like any herd of animals, we react together. That means that what one person does, we follow. If many people start suddenly buying a stock, many more people will join in, even without evaluating the quality of the asset or predicting its trend. This is what happened with the famous Theranos scandal; many people bought into a stock, but had no proof that it was actually based on anything. As a result, the losses were staggering when Theranos was exposed.

Finally, money for us is emotional and any type of investment comes with its own emotional baggage. Maybe you just want to be able to pay your bills, take a nice vacation, pay for your children's college tuition, etc. All of these emotional connections will impact your investments and the investments of others. In the event of a loss, this can cause a person to put more and more into investments in an attempt to regain their loss. Or when they've reached a high, they may keep trying to go even higher to make as much as they can for their goals. Either way, these actions impact the stock market and investments for everyone. If you can understand where people are coming from in their investment decisions, it might be easier to predict where the market will shift.

However, just like technical analysis and fundamental analysis, this isn't an exact science. It's easier to be aware of your own behavioral reactions and limit them, rather than trying to guess everyone else's behavior. If you're aware that you've reached your goal, then sell your stock. If you're taking a massive loss, get out, take a break, and try again. Don't keep pouring money into a ship that's already sinking. All of this can help you become a better swing trader.

In conclusion, swing trading is a great option for beginner traders. It gives you the chance to get your feet wet with a system of trading that has less risk than day trading. It's still risky, as all investments are, but if you approach it from a knowledgeable point of view, you'll be able to make some profit. Swing trading also gives you immediate feedback for your trades, unlike long-term investing. By using technical analysis, fundamental analysis, and some behavioral economics, you can analyze your swing trading opportunities and pick the ones best suited for you. In the next chapter, we'll discuss the pros and cons of swing trading before discussing other types of assets you can trade beyond stock.

Chapter Two: Swing Trading Pros and Cons

When we first look for a house or car to buy, we often take the time to look at the pros and cons. After all, there is a large amount of money involved and it wouldn't do to just walk up, pick a house, and pay for it without knowing the good and the bad of it. Like all things, swing trading has pros and cons too. Just like when buying a house or car, you need to take the time to analyze whether swing trading is right for you before dedicating time and money to it. This chapter will cover some of the pros and cons of swing trading. No trading type is without its risks, so it's important for you to take the time to analyze the pros and cons of swing trading before starting with your capital.

The Pros of Swing Trading

In the previous chapter, we talked a bit about some of the pros of swing trading. However, the pros are numerous. Keep in mind that while these aspects of swing trading are very positive, there is still risk involved in trading. Don't get the wrong idea about that, based on the list of pros. Here are six pros of swing trading.

1. Swing trading takes less time out of your day than day trading. This was touched on briefly in the previous chapter. Day trading requires you to focus intensely on your trade. In the matter of seconds to hours, your trade will come to an end, so it requires constant vigilance and no distractions. Swing trading isn't like this. With swing trading, you can still have a full-time job or other commitments without worrying about the small minute changes to your investments. You still need to give it some focus, but not to the same extent as day trading. With day trading, you need to take the time in your day to analyze the charts, and keep abreast of every update. Some day-traders can do it part-time or after work, but as a swing trader, you don't have to worry about this. When swing trading, you can do all of your analysis over the weekends, and schedule your trades then. Throughout the week, you can quickly check the charts to see how things are going and then choose your exit point. It's a lot less time consuming during your work week.

2. Swing trading will provide you with lower risks and quick rewards. Swing trading uses those short, small "swings" in a chart to make profits. This means you get maximum profits in a small amount of time. Because your cost-per-trade is lower than other types of investing, your risks are minimized. Lower risks and quick returns are definitely a

pro. But it only remains a pro if you are careful with how much you are putting on each trade so that your risks remain low. Higher cost-per-trade means higher risks.

3. Swing trading uses technical analysis. In the first part of the book, we looked at the different types of analysis used in swing trading. Technical analysis is what's used most frequently in swing trading and it saves you a considerable amount of time. It also simplifies the process of swing trading, as you don't have to go into the background of a company unless you want to.

4. Swing trading is very emotionally gratifying. Earlier, we looked at behavioral economics. Swing trading fits perfectly into our own behavior because humans like instant gratification. We love the challenge and the win of the trade. With swing trading, you get that gratification very quickly. Within a couple of days or weeks, and if you traded well, you'll get your reward.

5. Swing trading gives you a wide variety of assets you can trade. You can choose to work with stocks, options, or even bitcoin for swing trading. This variety is a pro because it means you're not limited as a trader. It also provides you with some diversification. Just remember to know the market you're going to be trading in.

6. This is probably one of the best pros for swing trading: there are a massive number of resources available to swing traders. There are apps you can use to trade, online spaces to chat with other traders, and so many blogs and websites with educational videos. Beyond this, there are also many websites you can use to practice your swing trades before putting any real capital into it. The number of resources available can really make it easy to step into swing trading. Which is why, once again, swing trading is perfect for beginner traders.

The Cons of Swing Trading

What goes up must go down, and like most things in the world, there is always a con. Swing trading is no different.

1. Overnight or weekend changes can decimate your investment. Because swing traders work over a longer period of time, that means that their assets continue to move even after the closing of the market. What that means for a trader is, that while you're asleep, your stock or asset can move in the opposite direction you want it to. If you're not careful and don't have a stop-loss in place, or an options contract to hedge your investment, you can

lose a lot of money. This is one of the biggest risks with swing trading. We'll talk more about stop-losses and options in later chapters.

2. It's possible to miss out on larger trends. Swing traders move fast. They don't stick around to see how a trade will pan out months or years from this moment. Because of this, they can miss out on larger trends and massive gains. Long-term investments take advantage of the possibility of long trends, but swing trading misses this opportunity. However, swing traders can still make decent profits, even if they jump off the bandwagon too early. They can also jump right back on if they want to.

3. You have to stay on top of all of your trades. Swing trading isn't a set-and-forget type of investment. It's not a house that sits quietly and slowly appreciates while no one lives there. It's a fast-paced, ever-changing investment strategy. Because of this, you have to make sure you are staying on top of your trades. This can take some time out of your hard-earned weekends, but the results can be worth it. If you forget your trades, you may lose more money than you intended to.

4. Your capital is tied up for a longer period. Most people don't have infinite capital, though there are a lucky few who seem to. Since swing trading requires a couple of

days, weeks, or months on set investments, it means that your capital is utilized for a longer period. It also means that you can't use that capital for other investments. If you plan out your investments and capital properly, then you can avoid this con by only having a small portion of your account active on swing trades.

5. High commission costs. Swing trading is all about frequent trades. However, these frequent trades can result in high commission costs. Therefore, if you plan on trading often, be prepared to also pay the commission costs for each trade.

6. Swing trading isn't suitable for volatile markets. In a very volatile market, swing trading is difficult. This is because, while there are many "swings" to trade in, there is no way to anticipate where the market will go next. You could have several assets that are looking good at the close of the trading day, and by the next morning, they could be completely gone. In a very volatile market, swing trading is not the best option, so it would be better to take on a different trading strategy during these points.

Chapter Three: Investment and Trading Opportunities

In the last couple of chapters, we've looked at swing trading and how it differs from other types of trading. In this chapter, we're going to look at the different assets you can trade. Some of these are ideal for swing trading, while others are not very ideal. Keep in mind that with swing trading, we're looking at liquid assets, that is, assets that are easily converted into cash.

Most people know that investing and trading can happen with stocks. That's what we learn from most of the movies we watch, the websites we view, and news we read. Stocks are a liquid asset and are perfect vehicles for swing trading.

However, there are many different asset choices for investment beyond stocks. These include bonds, mutual funds, options, and more. In this chapter, we'll go over some of the choices for investment.

Different Investment Opportunities

Stocks

Stocks are great for swing trading because you can purchase them individually and manage them yourself. However, they are also fairly risky. Stocks are, essentially, a small piece of a corporation's success. When you buy a share, you are purchasing a small portion of that corporation. That doesn't mean you own the company. It just means that you are benefiting from its growth. The company, in turn, uses that money to continue to fund their goals. If you own enough shares in a company, you can participate in their shareholder meetings. You might even receive some of the company's profits, though that's not guaranteed. If you buy most of the shares in a company that will give you controlling interest in the company and you will get to choose members of the board. But for most everyday investors, this isn't important. For swing traders, this is even less important. Swing traders don't care about the long-term value of the company. They simply want to buy a share during a "swing" in the company's numbers and get out quickly with a little bit of profit.

The value of the stock is based on the company's value so as the company's value increases, so too will the stock value. It works the same in the opposite direction as well. In the event that the corporation goes bankrupt, your assets are not in danger, though theirs are. Even though you won't be penalized for any bankruptcy in the company, you'll still be affected. The stock value will plummet, which means that what shares you have will also drop in value. If you're not quick enough to see the writing on the wall, you can lose a lot of money because you'll only be able to sell the shares at a greatly reduced price. On the flip side, if the corporation takes off and becomes extremely successful, the stock value will also drastically increase and the shares you own could make you a millionaire. Both of these scenarios are more likely with long-term investment than with day or swing trading. With stocks, your investment is a medium risk/high reward style of investing. Of course, it depends on what corporations you're purchasing shares from, but generally, stocks have a medium level of risk. If you want to work with less risk, then you should invest in bonds.

Bonds

In the U.S., it's really common for a person to take out a credit card or loan when they need the money. In exchange for issuing the loan or card, banks make a profit off of the interest you pay. Bonds are very similar to this system, except instead of a bank issuing the loan, you are. Often times a company or other entity needs to borrow money for their operations. Maybe the city needs new roads, or a company needs an influx of cash for a new product design. However, instead of asking a bank for a loan, a lot of times they will choose to issue bonds to the public for investors. Investors can, then, buy the bonds. A bond has the set price that you pay which will go to the company, the maturity date (when they'll pay you back), and the interest the company will pay you for your loan. A bond is not like a stock at all.

With a stock, a company takes the money you used to buy the share to fund their operations. In exchange, you get to revel in the company's success with increased share value or mourn in its demise. With a bond, you are agreeing to give a company money, but they must pay you back. You officially become a creditor to the company and they are legally required to pay you back with interest.

You might be familiar with the term "war bonds". Maybe your parents or grandparents had some. War bonds are bonds sold to citizens of a country in order for the government to raise funds for war. When the war is over, citizens get paid back (for the most part). Bonds can be issued by federal and state governments, corporations, cities, and companies. Really any large entity that needs an influx of cash can issue bonds. Once you have bought a bond, you don't have to keep it until it matures. Most people choose to keep the bond. However, bonds can be traded to other investors, or even be bought back by the issuing entity, which can earn you more profit. Bonds can be considered low risk, mostly because if the issuer goes bankrupt, creditors like the bondholders get paid out of the selling of assets. Government bonds are even less risky since the U.S. government is capable of paying back the bond bearers.

Bonds sound amazing, and they are if you want a low-risk investment. However, they're not ideal for swing trading because they're not nearly as liquid as stock investing. They also usually require more capital to purchase. That being said, bonds are an excellent opportunity for diversification which will lower the risk to your total account. We'll talk more about diversification in later chapters.

Mutual funds

When you were a kid, did you ever get dared to do something, but you refused to do it until your friends did it too? Somewhere along the line, we've learned that if more than one person is doing something, then everything will work out ok. Mutual funds play on this idea because it is essentially a group of investors coming together to purchase stock. However, it's not just one security. It's usually a mix of hundreds of stocks, bonds, and other assets. With mutual funds, the person who controls the funds and purchases the stock is the money manager of the fund. There is considerably less individual power involved in mutual funds than in purchasing individual securities. However, because they have so many assets purchased under one fund, they're very diversified which can help with your risk management. Another benefit of a mutual fund is that they're perfect for someone who wants a professional to manage their investments.

Mutual funds are different from stocks and bonds. With a stock, you're purchasing part of a company, and with a bond you're loaning money to a company. But when you purchase a share in a mutual fund, you are buying a portion of its portfolio. The portfolio might have stocks and bonds within it, but they're not owned by you. You simply own a bit of the portfolio itself. You won't receive funds as quickly as you would with trading individual stocks, but you'll receive a distribution from your mutual fund and you can choose to take the cash, or buy back into the mutual fund for more shares. You can also choose to leave the fund whenever you want, and you'll receive a distribution minus the commission costs involved.

In mutual funds, all investors gain and lose together. However, losses can be considerably lower than if you had a share in the individual stock. For example, if you invest in Facebook and they have a bad quarter, your shares in stock will decrease and cause you some grief. Maybe you paid $126 for a share, but now the share value is $100. That means you've lost $26 a single share. In a mutual fund, you'll only see a very small decrease in the values since a mutual fund is so diversified. This is beneficial for investors because it means you'll lose less money, therefore there is less risk in mutual funds. However, this risk depends on the management of the funds. If the assets are all purchased in one industry, this isn't very diversified and results in higher risk. Also, some mutual funds purchase assets in new industries, which means there is a higher chance of loss. Finally, if your money manager isn't legit, you could lose everything. However, this isn't common. So mutual funds can be a medium risk/medium reward investment.

You can, in theory, swing trade mutual funds, but that would require a lot of capital. Mutual funds have many fees associated with them, and if you swing trade, you'll have to pay those fees, since you'll be leaving the mutual fund earlier than its terms. You'll also be affecting the other shareholders with quick buying and selling. This can result in very high fees and even your account being blocked from making more trades. Therefore, while you can swing trade with mutual funds, it's not recommended.

Options

Options can be a little confusing, not only because of what they are, but because of how the word itself is used in English. In the English language, we use the word "options" to talk about possibilities. It's a verb. However, when discussing trading, we are using the options as its own thing, a noun. As this section and the next chapter explore options, remember that we're not discussing choices or possibilities, but another type of asset, like stocks.

Options are contracts for stocks or other assets, where you can buy or sell those assets at a predetermined price before the contract ends. Options are very different from stocks, bonds, and mutual funds. Instead of being a security itself, it is a contract for securities. The amazing part about options is that the price of the option itself is usually considerably lower than the price of the stock.

To help make options a little clearer, think about this example: when you're leasing a car, you sign a contract that gives you the rights to the car, but you only pay a fraction of the price that the car is valued at. After a certain point, your contract expires and you can choose to purchase the car at its set value, or have the contract end. Options are very similar to this scenario, because the car is the underlying asset and the leasing contract is the option.

Because options can be so cost-efficient, they are a good choice if you would like to buy 100 shares at a lower price. In the U.S., options are usually sold with 100 shares underlying the contract. While options can have stock underlying it, they are not like stocks because they don't give you part ownership of a company, nor do they pay you a dividend from the company. However, if you want these rights, then you can fulfill the contract and buy the shares at the set price.

Options are a good investment vehicle because they can be used to generate income and even hedge a loss during a downswing. To make an income of options trading involves selling your option for the set price to a buyer. This gives you extra capital, while transferring the risks of the stock price changes to the buyer. You can use swing trading to do this, by selling the options as the price of the stock is low, and then purchasing the same "sell" option (also called a put) when the price is high again. This will give you consistent income in a volatile market.

Options, in general, are fairly risky. In fact, there is an entire organization dedicated to educating consumers about options so that everyone is aware of the risk and rewards associated with options trading. Some people consider options to be a lower risk than stocks because you can exit them at any time. However, others consider them to be riskier because if you forget about a stock, you might still make a profit, but if you forget about an option, you can lose all the money you used to purchase it.

Additionally, as the writer of an option, you can face nearly unlimited loss.

There are several terms that must be understood in order to understand options: premium, strike, call, put, exercise, and expiration.

- Premium. The cost of the option contract itself is called a premium. Premiums can look pretty cheap, but remember that they're for 100 shares of stock, so you need to multiply their cost by 100. A premium is not a fixed price because as the option goes closer and closer to the expiration date, it will decay and drop in price. This is because it is unlikely for the stock to move in the required direction during the time left on the contract. Premiums are also not fixed because they depend a lot on stock value too. Basically, a premium is dependent on supply and demand. If you purchase an option at one premium, you need to be aware of its ever-changing future numbers.

- Strike. The set price of the underlying stock in the option is called the strike. For example, if the stock is originally selling for $60 per share, then the option might have the strike price at $50 per share. This price is what you would pay for the stock if you choose to fulfill the options contract.

- Call option. A call option is a contract that gives the holder the right to buy the underlying stock at the strike price, within a specified period of time. This is a right, not an obligation to buy. Often times, investors will sell the call option to another investor, rather than fulfilling the option and buying the stock. A call option works a bit like this: if someone has a call option with strike at $10 and the stock price is originally at $9, when the option expires and the stock has increased in value to $20, then the holder of the option can purchase the valued stock at $10 giving them additional profit. If you buy a call, you want or are expecting the stock to increase. Otherwise, it's worthless.

- Put option. A put option is a contract that gives the holder the right to sell the underlying stock at the strike price, within a specified period of time. Again, just like with a call option, this is a right, not an obligation to sell. Put options can be used to hedge your current stocks against a drop-in value. For example, if you have a put option on your stock, which is valued at $20 and your strike is $18, then if the stock decreases to $9 you can sell that stock for $18, providing you with a profit and a "safety net" since you would have otherwise lost $11 without the option. If you buy a put, that means you want or are expecting the stock to go down. If the stock goes up, your put is then worthless.

- Exercise. No, this term doesn't mean going to the gym, lifting weights, and trying to look glamorous while sweating. To exercise an option means that you are using it and will buy or sell the stock agreed upon in the contract. You will essentially fulfill the contract before it expires. You can use the option at any point before the expiration date, so you don't have to wait to exercise it until the last day.

- Expiration. This word is pretty obvious because it's the same word used for everything. When the option date is done and the contract can no longer be exercised, it's expired. Your option then becomes worthless and you may have no profit and some losses, depending on the way things turned out with the stock values. Most options expire on the third Friday of their expiration month. It's important to know that the expiration date is the last trading day for the options. For example, if it says March 20th, then March 20th is the last day you can exercise the option, not March 19th.

- In the money (ITM). Being in the money is when the strike price is working in the right direction of your trade. This depends on whether you are buying a call option or a put option. With a call option, in of the money means that the strike price is less than the underlying stock price. For example, if the strike price is $15 per share, but each share is selling for $20, then this is in the money because it's likely that the stock will be higher than the strike price, even if it dips a bit down. Remember, the goal of a call option is for it to rise higher than the strike price so that you are making a profit. With the strike price lower than the current stock price, it's likely that the value will rise high enough to meet and exceed your strike price. With a put option, in the money means that the strike price is more than the stock price. For example, if the strike price is $25, and the underlying stock is $20 per share, this is in the money. Remember, with put, you're hoping that the number goes lower than your strike price, so at this point it's in the money because it's likely that the stock will be reduced to below your strike price.

- At the money (ATM). When the strike price and the underlying stock price are the same, this means the option is at the money.

- Out of the money (OTM). Out of the money is when the strike price is starting in the wrong direction of your trade. This depends on whether you're buying a call option or a put option. With a call option, out of the money means that the strike price is more than the underlying stock price. For example, if the strike price is

$20 per share, but each share is selling for $15, then this is out of the money because it's unlikely that the stock will rise higher than the strike price. Remember, the goal of a call option is for it to rise higher than the strike price so that you are making a profit. With the strike price placed more than the current stock price, it's unlikely that the value will rise high enough to meet and exceed your strike price. With a put option, out of the money means that the strike price is less than the stock price. For example, if the strike price is $20, and the underlying stock is $25 per share, this is out of the money. Remember, with put, you're hoping that the number goes lower than your strike price, so at this point it's out of the money because it's unlikely that the stock will be reduced to below your strike price.

Options are a good choice for swing traders because you can make a profit and income during the swing prices of stock but with a reduced amount of capital. In the next chapter, we will discuss more about options trading.

Chapter Four: Details about Options

As a swing trader, trading options may sound a little complicated. But with enough understanding of how calls and puts work, you can make a good profit with trading options instead of directly trading stocks. Now that we know the basics of options, let's look at the call and put options in more detail.

Call and Put Options

As explained earlier, there are two types of basic options that you can buy: call and put options. Again, remember, while in English these two words are verbs, in this discussion they are a noun, a type of option. Call options give you the right to buy the stock at a set price, while put options give you the right to sell stock at the set price.

Call Options

A call option gives the bearer the right to buy an asset at the strike price but they don't have an obligation to buy those assets. Call options give you a lot of leverage because you can buy an option for 100 shares at a margin of the price, thus leveraging a bigger return. Call options are like a down payment. Let's explore an example based on the housing market.

If you live in an up and coming area, there will be new buildings. If you want to buy into a new condominium that isn't built yet, you can often negotiate the price beforehand and pay that for the condominium. Maybe you negotiate to pay $300,000 for the condo, this price may be based on the current housing market, the estimated future value, or the amenities that come with it. Either way, once you have agreed to pay $300,000 upfront, this is your contracted price. You'll own the condo at this price no matter what fluctuations occur. The contract may have an expiration of date, maybe of 3 years: this will give you the opportunity to move into the condo within 3 years. The condo's construction is completed in one year, and is valued at $800,000. Even though you only paid $300,000, you will still get the condo because that is your contracted and originally negotiated price. And you now have a massive profit on your hands.

With this big of a gap, you can turn around and sell the condo again to receive that profit in cash. However, if the condo is finished and is valued at only $100,000, then you have lost the cost of your contract, and your contract is virtually worthless. Even the contract is worthless to you now, it may increase in value over the next couple of years. If you still have time left on the contract, you may choose to keep it with the hopes of the condo's value increasing. If your three years are nearly over, and you choose not to exercise the contract, then you lose all of the money you have paid for the contract. This is how call options operate.

This last example is pretty straight forward, but it does show the inherent risks involved with options. If the stock prices change too much, you can lose the premium that you paid for the option. And while my example showed a huge profit, in reality, your profits will not be nearly as large when doing options trading. Let's look at an actual options trading example with our fake stock, ABC.

ABC stock is currently trading at $100 per share. You purchase a call option with the premium price of $3 and the strike price of $90. If, when nearing the options expiration date, ABC stock increases in value to $110, then you can exercise the option. Your profit will be the stock value minus the strike price, plus premium price. It looks like this: $110-($90+3) which equals $17. This $17 is your profit for one share. An option covers 100 shares, so your profit is $1700. However, if ABC stock is trading at less than the strike price, you lose the whole premium for that option. In this situation, the strike price is $90 and if ABC's value drops below $90, you will lose your $3 premium. This doesn't seem like a lot, but remember, the premium price has to be multiplied by 100 because the option covers 100 shares. Then, you would lose $300.

Put Options

Put options give the bearer the right to sell an asset at the strike price. Again, this isn't an obligation to sell, just a right. Put options are very similar to insurance. Here's a real-world example based on car insurance. Congratulations on buying your new Maserati! With such a gorgeous, expensive car it makes sense that you want to have car insurance. Let's say the car is valued at $100,000 and you purchase insurance that will cover your car for damage. The insurance company agrees to cover your car for $90,000 if the car is damaged within a period of 6 months. Of course, you are paying your insurance premiums, which might cost you $100 a month. Within those 6 months, if the car isn't damaged at all, then what you've paid for insurance is useless. It's nice to have it as a preventative measure, but it means you get nothing other than a safety net out of it. If, however, you total your car while trying to get to work, then you can go to your insurance company and demand restitution. Your insurance will give you the $90,000 to cover your car because that's the amount they agreed to. This is obviously better than receiving $0 which is what you would have had if you didn't have insurance on the car.

This situation is very similar to a put option, where the premium for the option is $100, the strike price is $90,000, and the stock value is $100,000. In this situation, you make a profit when the car is totaled because you are gaining money minus the premium price, when you would have originally received nothing. This is what a put option is. You can use a put option to hedge the stocks that you currently own. This way, if the stock value dips below what you originally paid for them, you can still walk away with a decent price. Here's another example with our fake stock, ABC.

Stock ABC is currently trading at $219 per share. An investor believes that the stock is unlikely to drop very far, so to ensure that don't lose money from an unexpected drop, he buys a put option for $.80 with a strike price of $200. Within a month, and before the options expiration date, ABC's stock value drops to $190 per share. The investor can choose to exercise his put option, purchasing the shares at $190 and selling them to the put option writer for $200. This gains the investor a profit of $10 per share and a total of $1000 minus commission costs and the premium cost. The further the shares of ABC drop, the more profit the put options owner can make. However, the put options writer can lose a substantial amount of money.

The writer gets the premium price, which they often use for income, and hopes that the shares don't drop so they don't lose out. In this situation with a drop-in share price, the put option writer is obligated to purchase the shares at the agreed upon price of $200 even though they're only valued at $190. The put option writer is then out, and losses $1000 ($10 per share) with the potential to lose the entirety of the value, $20,000 if the stock value dropped to $0.

The risk in this situation is very high for the writer of the option. Therefore, it's a good idea to be the one buying options instead of writing them. While writing options can give you a steady income, if you predict the stock's movement wrong, your losses can be nearly unlimited.

Options Trading Pros and Cons

As we've seen from the examples above, a lot of profit can be made from buying and exercising options, whether call or put. However, there is also some risk involved. If done well, your losses will only include the cost of the premium, but if you're writing the option, your losses can be unlimited. In this section, we'll explore some of the pros and cons of options trading.

Pros of trading options

We've already seen some of the pros associated with options trading, but here is a comprehensive list. Even though there are substantial pros, keep in mind the risks associated with options trading. Do not assume there are no risks involved. Here are the pros associated with options:

- Options trading can be very cost-efficient. Let's say that you want to buy 100 shares of stock ABC. At $200 per share, that's $20,000 in capital. If you're just starting out in trading, that's a daunting amount. Instead, you could purchase a call option for $1. That $1 has to be multiplied by 100 (for the 100 shares). The premium is a total cost of $100. $100 is far less costly than $20,000 but for the same number of shares. This is a lot of leverage that can lead to greater profits than buying the stock alone. Beyond the buy-in price, options trading is cost-efficient because it only requires a margin trading account, so you don't need to have a full account to trade with options. Therefore, options trading is a great possibility if you want to use less capital.

- Buying options is less risky than buying stock alone. Continuing with the example from the previous point, let's say that you did, in fact, spend $20,000 on 100 shares of ABC stock. Then, the market crashes and your

100 shares are now worth $1000. That's a massive loss and you probably won't be able to get it back. With options, this won't be a problem. If you have a pull option, then you can exercise it, buy the shares at $10 each, and receive the difference when you sell the shares to the put writer for the strike price. Your profit is then massive. If you have a call option, it is now, unfortunately, worthless but all that you have lost is the premium amount, $100. This is a better loss than the $19,000 you would have lost if you bought the stock directly.

- Options provide you with the same return as someone who has invested in stocks. If a trader buys a share of stock for $200 and the share value increases to $300, then the shareholder makes a profit of $100. For the same shares, if an option holder purchases a call option for the same stock, with a strike of $200, and the stock rises to $300, they make the same profit.

- Options are flexible. You can trade options themselves, without exercising them, you can purchase calls and puts, or you can write them. You can do long calls/puts or short calls/puts. Really, there is a whole variety of things you can do with options. With stocks, the only options are to buy, hold, or sell them. There isn't much beyond that.

Cons of trading options

Nothing is without risks, and this includes options. Despite how marvelous they sound, and how much profit you can make from them, you need to know and understand the risks associated. In fact, there is an entire organization dedicated to educating buyers and making the risks with options clear. This organization is called the Options Industry Council. Their website is a massive resource for those who are interested in options buying and writing.

Here are some of the risks associated with options:

- Options have many moving parts you must keep track of. Even though options sound fairly straight forward, you have to maintain your focus on all the pieces. Remember that the premium costs change every day. Literally. Every day. As the option's expiration date comes nearer, the premium prices will shift and become lower. If you want to trade your options to other investors, you must be aware of the shifts in premium costs. Beyond watching the premium costs, you also need to remember the expiration date. If you forget, then you can lose the premium that you paid for the option. And then the final pieces are, of course, checking the stock prices regularly to see if you want to exercise the option. All of this comes together in a list of parts you need to regularly check and keep in mind.

- Options are influenced by many factors. This influence can lead to a change in the costs and the rewards you are hoping to get. The underlying stock influences the price of the option. It also, obviously, influences whether or not you want to purchase a call option or a put option. Choose the wrong option, and you can miss out on profits. But remember, as long as you are purchasing an option, the most you can lose is just the cost of the premium. The economy and the market itself can also impact the options. However, the economy and market influence all aspects of trading.

Chapter Five: Risk Management Strategies

With any investment plan must come some risk management strategies. All trading involves risk, and swing trading is no exception whether you are swing trading with stocks, options or other assets. However, most risks can be controlled so that you're never at risk of losing all of your funds. To ensure this doesn't happen to you, it's important to have a strategy and follow it. Without a strategy, you're more likely to take on more risk with your investments, which can lead to dramatic losses.

In general, most people know about diversification. However, having basic money management, using options to hedge your trades, and having a good mindset can also help you manage the risks associated with swing trading. We'll cover all of these topics in this chapter.

Diversification

Have you ever gone to Florida in the wintertime? If so, maybe you packed a swimsuit, beach towel, and sunscreen, but also brought along a sweater, boots, and a warm hat, just in case. This is diversification. If you're preparing to cover your bases on a vacation, then you're also prepared for diversification in your investing. While swing trading is really exciting and worthwhile, it's a good idea to broaden your investments beyond this. You can diversify your investments across investment strategies, assets, and industries.

At the beginning of this book, we discussed some of the different investment strategies like day trading, long-term investing, and swing trading. To diversify your investments, you can try different types of trading together. Doing both swing trading and day trading isn't recommended because of the heavy workload, but you can combine long-term trading or trend trading with either of those short-term trading options. Doing swing trading while also having a couple of long-term investments can be a great way to diversify your portfolio. This is because if anything happens to your short-term trading, your long-term investments can provide you with a backup. The opposite is also true. Most people already have some long-term investments with their 401ks or Roth IRA's. But having additional long-term investments beyond your swing trades offers you further flexibility. It can take a weight off your mind if you're hesitant about swing trading, because even if you fail with a swing trade, you'll still have funds from your long-term investments.

Another way to diversify is by investing with different assets. If you want to swing trade with stocks and options, then plan to have some other assets that are also being invested. This means investing in bonds or mutual funds as well as stocks and options. While this sounds like a lot, it really provides you with a safety margin. If your stocks reduce in value before you can trade them, your bonds will still be gathering interest. In the same way, if your options expire before you can off-load them or exercise them, then you'll still get an income from your mutual fund's divestment.

A good rule to use for diversifying your assets is to follow the rule of 110. In this rule, you take the number 110 and subtract your age. The final number is the percentage of your portfolio that should be in stocks. The rest should be diversified to other assets. For example, if your age is 35 then you would do the math like this: 110-35=75. This means that 75% of your portfolio should be stocks and 25% should be other assets like mutual funds, bonds, and other investments like real estate. However, if your risk tolerance is lower, then you should reduce the number of stocks in your portfolio to maybe 50-50. It is, of course, up to you how much risk you would like to take with your portfolio, but diversifying across assets is a great way to protect your money and your investments.

Buying assets and stocks across a variety of industries is another way to diversify. No matter which type of investment strategy you use, or which assets you choose to purchase, if you don't have everything diversified across industries, then you're setting yourself up for failure. Think of it like this: if you buy only assets within one sector, let's say the car industry, if that industry than suffers a loss as a whole, your entire portfolio goes down the tubes. That means all of your long-term investments, all of your swing trades, every mutual fund or bond you own in the sector, all of it will be decimated if the industry collapses. Thus, it's important to diversify across industries. Pick assets from industries you're interested in, ones that have steady growth, or ones that are just typically steady. Think about which industries will still be around in the future or industries that supply basic human needs. These are the ones that are going to be the most consistent. If you want to swing trade in a more volatile market, choose industries that are always changing like technology ones or energy. Just keep in mind to diversify between industries. So, you can swing trade in technology, but have a long-term investment in textiles.

If you diversify with these three different aspects, then your portfolio is sure to bring you some benefits. It will also reduce your overall risk while you swing trade.

Basic Money Management

Having some basic money management skills can help you reduce your risks while swing trading. Unlike diversification, these won't have literal monetary impacts on your portfolio. These tips are mostly to help you set up things in your daily life so that as you swing trade, you still maintain enough capital to live off of. Basic money management includes skills like knowing your debt and debt management, savings, your tolerance for risk, how much capital you have every month, and what percentage of that you're willing to put into the investment. Knowing basic money management can reduce your investment risk because it means that you know your exact financial situation and won't get yourself into financial trouble from poor trading.

Without money management skills, you may exceed your funds each month on trading. You may end up using your grocery money to fund your trades, or worse, rely on your trades for your grocery money. Therefore, having basic money management can ensure that all of your bases are covered and that your investments are not going to ruin your lifestyle.

If losing a trade makes your stomach drop and sweat break out on your body, then you're trading too much and you need to take a step back and analyze your finances. Are you trading to add a little extra to your income or are you trading for your entire livelihood? Swing trading can work as your income but only after months and sometimes years of consistent trading. Don't rely on it from the get-go. Most traders lose all of their investment funds within the first year of trading. Don't do that. You need to balance what you're investing with what you're living off.

A good way to balance your living expenses is to do the 50/30/20 rule. This rule divides your income into needs, wants, and savings. In the case of investing, that comes out of the "20" portion of your income. That means as a swing trader, you can put aside 20% of your income for trading, investing and other savings like an emergency fund. Another 50% of your income goes to your needs like rent, healthcare, and groceries. Whatever you do, don't dip into your "needs" portion of your financial plan because then you won't be able to cover your basic monthly needs. This can put added stress on you to make up the losses through trading, but that's not the right mindset to enter into trading with. The final 30% of your income goes to your wants like dates, hobbies, and eating out. By compartmentalizing your income in this manner, you can be sure not to exceed your budget for your trades.

Now, just because you've compartmentalized your income, doesn't mean that you'll follow it. Consequently, it's important to have the discipline necessary to follow your trading financial plan.

Hedging with Options

We've talked before about how put options can help you when a stock drops below a certain price. When doing swing trading, there is a considerable risk of the market changing overnight or over the weekends. If you're very worried about potential loss, you can buy a put option for your stock. That way if the market does drop, you can use sell your stock to the put option writer for the strike price on the option. You may still have some loss, but not as much as you would have had.

Changing your Mindset

The moment your livelihood or a specific event relies on investing, you become even more emotionally connected to your trades. This means that you might make emotional decisions which can result in steep losses in all aspects of your life. It's important to have the right mindset for trading. This is an essential risk management strategy. It may not sound like it, but your emotions can cause you to take on far more risk than you should. Having the right mindset can help mitigate the risks in your trades. It can also help you have a more winning mindset.

When you have been trading for a while, or even just starting out, it's important to keep your attitude about the market positive. If you act like the market is out to get you, then it causes you more fear about your trades, and a lot of self-doubt. The market isn't out to get you, though it's easy to feel that way. When you start feeling like this, it's a good time to take a step back and reevaluate your objectives and goals. It also might be a good point to take a break to regain your confidence in the market.

Most importantly, this is the point when you should practice with a simulator, because it is your emotions that are getting in the way of your successful trades. If your feelings about the market remain negative, it's very likely that you'll keep pushing in more money, and getting more losses because of it so it's important to step back if necessary and this will help you to manage the risks of trading.

To do well while trading, it's important to have a lot of self-confidence. If you have confidence in your skills as a trader, then you won't be shaken when you have some failures. Notice how I wrote, "when". That's because everyone who trades has a failure at some point. Having a lot of self-confidence means that you won't become too emotionally connected to your trades. As mentioned earlier, being too emotionally invested in your trades can result in a lot of losses as you pour money into your trades. Self-confidence can be a good risk management strategy.

Another good mindset that can help with risk management, is training yourself to be flexible and adaptable. The markets are always changing. They never stop changing. Therefore, it's important as a trader to also change with the markets. If a strategy isn't working, change it up to a new strategy. If you're facing some losses, then try something else or spend some time practicing in a simulator. Being flexible and adaptable means that you won't keep trading when you are taking on more and more losses. It means that you know when it is time to try something new. This will help to lower your risks in trading.

Two aspects that you will have to work on for risk management is overcoming your fear and controlling your greed. It's easy to feel some fear while trading. After all, seeing the charts dip can be frightening, especially because it's your money that's falling. However, if you let your fear control you then you may not go back into trading once you've been hit with a loss. It's important to overcome your fear and get back into trading. On the opposite side of this coin is controlling your greed. Often, traders will see a stock rising higher and higher, and instead of exiting to take what profit they can, they remain with the stock. But everyone knows that no trade remains in a pattern of always going higher. There is always a downswing. Learn to control your greed of the markets and exit when you planned on exiting. This will help you lower your risks when trading.

Controlling Addictions

Trading is like gambling. We've discussed this a bit before, but here it is reiterated again: Trading is like gambling. And like any type of gambling, it's very important that you know when enough is enough and when a new strategy is needed. It is important that when you trade, you have control of all of your emotions, but beyond this, it's really important not to get addicted. If you become addicted to trading, then you'll take more risks, spend more money, and experience more loss. It is critical that trading doesn't become something that dominates your life and all of your funds. Hence, controlling addictions or addictive tendencies is a crucial risk management strategy.

Now you may be thinking there's no way that a person can get addicted to trading, but this idea is wrong. Trading can be really gratifying. When you are successful at a trade, you will feel satisfied. And when you are not successful, you might feel a bit disheartened. However, with more trades, these emotions can become increased to the point where all that matters is the "win" and losses force you to make more trades to make up for them. The moment this happens, you're no longer making sound trading choices, and are instead acting out of a compulsion to keep making more trades.

In general, an addiction is categorized as something that interferes with your daily life, brings you a certain amount of shame, gives you an adrenaline rush, takes up all of your thoughts and ruins your relationships. Let's go over how this might look if you are addicted to trading.

- Trading interferes with your daily life. Important aspects of daily life include keeping up with your routines, eating meals, maintaining relationships, keeping appointments, etc. If swing trading is interfering with your daily life, then it means you might be spending all day focused on your trades. If you're missing out on daily tasks so that you can trade, then it's interfering with your life. This includes spending an inordinate amount of time glued to your phone, missing meals because you're too focused, or choosing to trade over healthy habits. If you can't pick your kids up from school because you're too busy watching the charts, then it's moved past an investment strategy and is now more of an addiction.

- Trading brings you some shame. You know if you're using all of your time and mental energy on trading. Your family might even know and it's likely that they'll try and get you to take a break from trading. But more than likely, you'll keep on trading anyways. You might feel ashamed about this and hide it from your family. When your friends walk in on you, you might quickly hide the charts on your phone, or quickly change to another app. If you feel some shame about how much you are trading, and make extraordinary efforts to hide your trades, then you may have a problem.

- Trading gives you an adrenaline rush. While it's quite normal to be happy when you've successfully made a trade, problems can occur when it suddenly becomes an adrenaline rush. This is because adrenaline never stays, so you have to keep taking bigger and bigger risks to get the same feeling again. Obviously, this can result in a lot of financial difficulties. If you are constantly seeking that rush from trading, then you definitely need to take a step back. At that point, it's likely that trading may have become a problem for you.

- Trading takes up all of your thoughts. Have you ever had something in your life that you loved so much, it literally dominated your thoughts? Maybe it was that new video game that was coming out, or a new relationship. Usually, after a certain point, that domination eases. But if it doesn't, then it becomes a problem. If your swing trades are taking up all of your thoughts, preventing you from sleeping, or causing you undue stress, then you may want to take a step back from trading. If you can't take that step back, then your trading may be an addiction.

- Trading ruins your relationships. This one is an addictive trait that can really just destroy everything. As humans, we long for relationships. This doesn't just mean romantic relationships but also friendships, siblingships, etc. So, if something comes in the way of making and keeping relationships, that's a problem. If trading starts to dominate everything and results in you neglecting your relationships, then trading is the problem.

All of these aspects mentioned are a basic part of all addictions, not just trading addictions. If you see any of these behaviors while trading, then you may be addicted to trading. Again, addictions cause you to take more risks with trading and also damage your life beyond trading. Thus, controlling any addictions is one of the most important means of risk management. Luckily, if you're addicted to trading, there are ways to get help. You can work with a therapist, or join a Gamblers Anonymous group. If you hesitate to do any of these, you can talk with your doctor or call the National Problem Gambling Council's helpline. This call center is completely anonymous and can provide you with more resources to help. The number is 1-800-522-4700.

Chapter Six: Swing Trading with Call Options

In the last few chapters, we've learned a lot about swing trading, different types of assets to trade and risk management. Now it's time to go into the "how's" of swing trading. This chapter and the next one will discuss how to swing trade stocks and options, as well as how to look at charts to find patterns, and how to make a trading plan. Once you are finished with these chapters, please, don't just leave the book and start trading! Instead, take what you've learned and use some practice simulators to do some practice trades. You should spend time practicing before using your money to swing trade.

How to Swing Trade

Let's review some of the basics of swing trading. Swing trading is buying an asset during a "swing" in the chart. If you're looking at a chart, the swings are those short rises up and the short rises back down. They make the small hills and valleys in the chart. They're pretty small, so you're not looking for a larger trend, you're simply looking for those changes that occur during a week-long period. In swing trading, you need to analyze the chart, find the support and the resistance of the asset, and then determine a good area to enter and exit the trade. Your analysis will also show you where to place your stop-loss. A stop-loss is incredibly important because it can help you prevent you from over-investing in the trade. This sounds really simple, but there's more to it, so this section will cover these topics.

How to find the support and resistance

As a swing trader, you should sell the asset before it reaches the resistance. Resistance is the highest point reached before a reversal or swing low. It is the point at which most people start selling their stock, and thus, it starts a new dip in the trend. Support is the lowest point it reaches before going up. Support is the point at which many people start buying the stock, so the stock prices rise.

Take, for example, a person throwing a ball in the air. The point of your hands holding the ball before the throw is your support point. It is the lowest point that the ball reaches before you throw it. After throwing the ball, the highest point in its arch, before it falls again, is the resistance. When swing trading, you want to sell the asset before it reaches resistance.

The reason why you want to sell your stock before you reach resistance is because resistance is the area where most people start selling. This means that your stock price might dip soon after so it's a good idea to sell before you hit resistance. Resistance can be calculated by analyzing a chart. Look at the chart's history for the last year. What is the highest point the stock is valued at, and how consistent is that? For example, if you're trading stock ABC, and you look back at their last 12 months on the market, you want to find at which points they were selling the highest. Maybe for a couple of months out of the year, the highest value the stocks had was $20. If it's a consistent pattern, then that is your resistance level. It's unlikely that the stock will break out of this pattern. This means that you want to plan your exit before this number is reached.

Resistance can be a useful tool for determining the peak price of a stock, but so can be other tools like moving averages. Whichever tool you choose in order to find the topmost point, make sure you stick with it and don't trade beyond that point. One thing with swing trading is that you won't know if the stock will go beyond the resistance point, but you still need to have your exit plan and follow it.

Support is the point at which you may want to buy the stock. Remember, support is the historically lowest point on the chart where the stock has been placed. Using the same strategy as the resistance one, you want to look at a chart's history for the last twelve months and find the areas where the stock has traded the lowest. For example, if you're trading stock ABC and you see that for the last year, the stock never dipped below $10, then that would be your support line. You don't want to trade below these points. In fact, it would be better to enter the trade somewhere a bit higher and ride the wave of the swing to your exit point. Remember, the goal is to find small profits in a short period of time, so once you've planned your exit within a few days, take it. Even if the market is doing well, it's better to bow out early than mistime it and lose your profits.

Again, just like with resistance, you can combine the support line with the moving averages tool to help you find the points that are best to enter in. Most charts that you'll find online will include the choice to see the moving averages for both the highs and the lows. You can use resistance and support to help you calculate from there.

Now that you understand the basics of resistance and support, it's time to practice. Find a sample stock chart online. You can use stockchart.com or other websites. Stock charts are free, so you don't need to pay to see the data. Using your sample chart, draw your lines for support and resistance during a given point in time. As you draw your lines, keep some things in mind: support and resistance lines are often slanting, going in the direction of the trend. They're not always horizontal, though they can be if the market is neutral and there is no prevailing trend. Find the areas on the chart where there are multiple touches. For example, maybe the lines touch the price point $120 multiple times in the last year. This is a good place to put your resistance or support line (depending on how the rest of the chart looks). Within these two lines is now your zone for purchasing. You can find an area that you would enter the trade and an area that you would exit based on what you're seeing. This is just a practice, furthermore you have the benefit of seeing a past chart.

To apply this to a future trade, try the same thing, but this time analyze the charts of three different securities you're interested in. Map out your support and resistance, and then choose a place that you would enter into the trade and where you would like to exit the trade. Remember to exit before resistance, and enter after support. Using a simulator (remember, practice first), or just by following the chart for a couple of days, you can see how your trade would have panned out if you had put money on the trade. Keep practicing this way, and you'll be able to find patterns in the markets. Since, as mentioned before, history repeats itself when it comes to trades. You can also adjust your strategies regarding resistance and support after some trial and error.

Remember to take lots of time to practice trades with a simulator, or just by following your own charts for a while before using your capital. Once you're ready to actually start trading, you want to follow the strategy that you developed, and map out your resistance and support. In the next section, we're going to talk about pinpointing the best areas to enter and exit a trade.

When to enter and exit the trade

When you were a kid, did you ever play double Dutch jump rope? Double Dutch is where two people are swinging two ropes and a third person has to jump in for a bit before jumping out. As a kid, it was brutal and difficult to find the right timing to jump in without getting hit with a rope. Entering into a trade can be just as nerve-wracking. You can be setting up to enter the trade and stress yourself with questions like, "Do I jump in now? How about now?" But with some strategic planning, and practice, you can find the best area you would like to jump in on a regular basis.

The entry point in a trade is the point at which you want to buy an asset. It's the starting bid in your trade. Whether you are trading stocks or options, you will always have to have an entry point. Having a good plan for when you will enter into a trade is really beneficial because it means that you won't have to drive yourself mad. It also means that you won't be making an emotional choice regarding when to enter.

Choosing a good entry point means analyzing the chart for support, resistance, and trend. Look at the past movement of the chart and find the support and resistance. Then, look at the trend. Has the chart been moving in a specific trend line? Or has it been in a stage of consolidation? Or a period where the market has remained fairly steady? With a stock that has a trend line, you can choose a point right after a rebound. For example, let's say stock ABC was trading at $60 in November before dropping to $58. As the number starts to rise again, you can see if the chart seems like it's going to return to trend. If yes, then you can place your entry point at $60 and wait to see if the trend will continue upward.

In the case of a stock that is at a stage of neutral movement, then your support and resistance lines will be horizontal and the chart will remain between those two lines. In this case, follow the pattern of the previous movement and again place your entry point at the price where a rebound is likely to happen. This should be close to the support line. There's a good chance that the stock value will rise again towards the resistance in this case.

Let's put this into action. Chose two different practice charts. One should have a stock that is trending upwards, and one should have stock that is steady and isn't trending in a particular direction. Taking the one that is trending upward, draw the trend line in the support line position. From there, choose a position that offers you a small swing up. At what point would you enter the swing? At what price point? How long would you remain in the swing? Do the same for the chart that is remaining steady. What point above the support line would you enter into the trade? It's easy to do this with past charts because everything is already lined up. But take the time to analyze the chart. What makes specific swings more successful and what makes them unsuccessful? Now try with a practice future trade. Again, find a chart from a stock that you would be interested in purchasing. Map out your lines, find the zone you'll trade in, and then choose an entry point either in the present or the future. After that, watch the stock for the next several days. Would your trade have panned out? If yes, why? And if no, why not? All of this practice gives you the opportunity to try out trades before investing any capital into it. Once you feel a bit more confident about entry points, move on to learn about exit points.

Before we discuss exit points, there's one important thing that needs to be mentioned. When you enter into the trade, you need to make sure that your risk/reward ratio makes the trade worth it. Once you calculate the ratio, you can determine at what point you can exit the trade in order to make the reward worth it. We'll discuss risk/reward ratios in the "Picking the right trades" section.

Now we're going to learn how to exit a trade. It is very important to have an exit strategy. Without an exit strategy, you will choose to leave a trade whenever you feel like it, which can cause you some losses. You may exit too early or too late. It is better to have a strategy in place so that you know exactly when you'll exit. For example, if you determine that you would like to make a specific amount of profit, that's your exit point. Don't go past that.

Let's continue the analogy mentioned earlier about a ball. As you throw it, momentum keeps it going higher but at a slower pace until it reaches its peak. At this point, momentum is zero and the ball falls back to your hands. In a swing trade, you want to exit the trade before the momentum reaches zero. Not at the peak, but before the peak. This is because most traders will be looking to sell at the peak of the trade, which will cause a drop in the market. Selling early before the estimated peak is a risk. It might mean that you lose out if the ball continues to go much higher than you anticipated. However, you will still have made a gain before any reversal happens and you can always buy back into the trend if you want to.

When looking at the charts for a stock, you should keep in mind your entry position and where you would like to exit. If the stock has stayed steady over the last bit of time and remains in its range, then looking at the support and resistance can give you a good idea of where to exit. If you entered near the support, then you can determine at what point you would like to exit. This depends on a lot of factors like your tolerance for risk and how long you want to stay in the trade. Generally speaking, if the stock value keeps increasing, you want to exit before it hits the resistance. Remember, in swing trading, it's all about small gains, not large ones so it's better to leave with some profit rather than no profit.

- With your support and resistance marked on a chart, you can also look for key indicators that show you that it's time to sell. One of these indicators is either if the stock value exceeds its resistance, or if it drops below its support numbers. This can mean that it's starting to trend in one specific direction, but it could also mean that these little breakouts will backtrack into the range it was sitting at before. If the stock value exceeds its resistance and you haven't sold yet, then you can choose to wait until it returns to its range, or see if it will be the start of a new trend. This decision, again, depends on how much risk you're willing to take.

There are a couple of things you can do to make sure that you are not staying in a trade too long. The first one is to set a stop-loss. A stop-loss is a tool that will sell your shares in the event that the stock price goes too low. We'll discuss stop-losses in detail in a little bit. The other option is to set a limit order. A limit order will sell your trades once they've reached your set peak value. Let's say that the current stock price for ABC is $20 per share when you enter. You can choose to set your limit order at $25 a share. You can also set it at a certain percentage point for profit. This means that at the $25 mark, your broker will sell your shares. This can be good because it can limit your losses, but it can also prevent you from taking advantage of a possible trend. So once again, make a decision based on your tolerance for risk.

As you make your exit strategy, you should ask yourself a few questions. You should know how long you are willing to stay in a trade, how much risk you can tolerate and at what point you want to get out. These three things will help you make a good exit strategy. For example, when asking yourself how long you want to stay in a trade, you can think about how long you want your capital to be tied up, what indicators you're looking for that will cause you to sell, etc. When considering how much risk you're willing to take, try a few different scenarios. Also, consider what a profit is to you.

Is it a $1 per share a decent profit or do you want to make more? Finally, consider when you want to leave the trade. You should have this written down clearly. Are you going to leave the trade once you've made a certain profit, once you hit the resistance level, or once you see another indication that it's time to go? When you've made your plan, it's important you stick to it. This will help you remain emotionally objective when trading.

Once you've made your exit plan, it's time again to practice. Follow the same technique mentioned before. Look at some past charts and analyze where you would have entered and exited the trade, based on the indicators like support and resistance, or based on the moving average. Analyze every piece of a move. Why would a certain exit point have worked or failed? Afterwards, try this again with a future chart. You can either do this in a simulation or using your own chart website of choice. Pick a stock you want to follow and find an entry point you think will work for you. Then, using your exit strategy, determine when you will exit the chart. Spend a few days looking at your plan as the chart moves forward. Did your plan work? Are there other ways you could have executed it? Keep practicing, don't just do this with one chart and think you're ready to start trading.

Where to place your stop-loss and why

We've talked a little about stop-losses, but let's look at them in more detail and explore the different types you can use. A stop-loss is very similar to a fire alarm. The fire alarm in your house starts to go off the moment that it senses smoke. It doesn't have to be a literal fire for it to sound the alarm. This can be kind of irritating, but it is also a very close analogy of what a stop-loss is. And yes, on occasion a stop-loss can also be irritating if it's not set correctly. A stop-loss can help you sell your trades when the market turns in an unexpected direction. It's your warning system and safety net in one. It makes sure that if the market is going to drop, you aren't going to lose a massive amount of money. However, sometimes a stop-loss is placed too tight which results in it being triggered during regular market volatility. This is that annoying accidental fire alarm. Even though it can be annoying, a stop-loss can save you considerable grief. As a swing trader, your trades will cover some days and weekends, which can result in precarious nights where the market shifts unexpectedly. A stop-loss can help you ensure your losses aren't too steep.

For most people, the ideal place to set up a stop-loss is close to their entry point. If your exit is nearby, it's easier to escape from the fire unscathed. It's the same way with the market. If your stop-loss is near, you won't lose much if everything goes down the drain. That being said, you don't want your stop-loss to be so close that the slightest move in the market results in you being kicked out. Try to keep a balance of it being set close to the entry point, but also leaving room for some volatility.

Stop-losses come in many different varieties to best fit your needs. Beyond the basic stop-loss, there are three different variations: Good 'til canceled, day-order, and trailing stop.

Good 'til canceled orders sound exactly like their name. In few words, it's a stop-loss that you place and it won't be canceled until you manually cancel it, or when the conditions are met, in which case it executes the sell. They do come with expiration dates as a safety measure, so they're not held onto indefinitely. There are a couple of downsides to good 'til canceled stop-losses. Because they have to be canceled manually, sometimes traders have had it execute at points they didn't want them to. Also, sometimes they are triggered in volatile markets which results in the trader selling low and having to buy back high if they want to remain in the same stock. These two downsides are part of the reason why many exchanges won't allow good 'til canceled transactions. However, if you want one, most brokerage accounts will let you set that stop-loss in-house.

Day-order stop-losses aren't frequently used by swing traders. They're mostly used by day traders and, as the name suggests, they last only one day. If the price that will trigger the day order isn't met, then the order gets canceled automatically. This can set up some investors for failure if they don't realize their order is only for one day so if you are going to use a day-order, it's important that you are aware of its longevity. One positive aspect of the day-order is that you can use it as a limit order for your exit point. This means that once the asset reaches a specific value, your day-order can be triggered to buy or sell the asset. It's more than just a stop-loss.

The final type of stop-loss you can use is a trailing stop. It is set at a specific percentage point or dollar mark from the current stock price. It then trails the stock as it moves. Here's an example. You buy ABC long stock for $10 and set the trailing stop for 10%. As the stock price moves up, the trailing stop will follow up to the next peak. However, it doesn't move back down, so if the stock value decreases, the trailing stop won't move down with it. When the stock value meets the 10% margin of the trailing stop, the stop will execute, selling the shares.

This is just a basic example, but you can set the percentage difference of the trailing stop. A trailing stop is a good choice if you want more flexibility in your stop-loss. Something to keep in mind with using it, is that the set price or percentage shouldn't be too close to the stock value. In other words, you don't want a small downshift in the market to trigger the trailing stop to execute. You also don't want the reverse, with the trailing stop having too large a distance between it and the stock value. In this situation, it won't react appropriately to the changes in stock value. In both situations, you can be set up for a loss, so it's important to set your trailing stop in the right position.

Whichever type of stop-loss you choose, it's important to actually use it and set it up. A stop-loss can save you from a lot of heartache in your trades.

Picking the Right Trades: Swing Trading with Call Options

As a swing trader, you don't have the luxury of picking a stock or option and waiting on it for months, or sometimes years. Your goal is to do quick swings for quick profits. With this in mind, it's important to know the best trades to pick. It's also important to know your risk/reward for each trade so that you are making the right decisions.

When you are picking the right assets to trade, start off by knowing whether you want to trade options or stocks. Buying options is a great choice if you have limited capital to work with. It provides you with a lot of leverage to get the same returns as if you had bought the stocks themselves.

When trading options, it's best to purchase call options and work with those. In this situation, we're not talking about writing options. While writing options can give you a decent income, they can also result in nearly unlimited losses. Buying call options, on the other hand, can give you potentially unlimited gains. Surprisingly, most swing traders don't exercise their options. Instead, they sell the options again to other investors. In this way, swing traders benefit from the option's premiums and are not liable for the underlying stock.

Trading options in this manner can be a little difficult. You have to keep track of the changes to the premium prices. These changes are based on how the underlying stock changes in value, the time before expiry, as well as other economic factors. The best bet with trading options is to trade them quickly and get the small gains in the premium that may result from a change in the market. If you hold onto your options too long, you may not be able to trade them for a profit, but if the opportunity presents itself, you could always exercise the options for a gain in that situation.

If you want to trade stocks instead of options, then choose ones that have the most swings in a short amount of time. This doesn't mean highly volatile markets. Just choose ones that are actively traded. Large-cap stocks are some of the most actively traded stocks so they have the most swings during a week. You can use those swings to make a profit. Large-cap stocks are for companies that have a huge amount of capital.

Think Apple, Microsoft, and Facebook. Other companies might include gas and oil companies, large tech companies, etc. These companies tend to be very consistent and without a lot of volatility. They're the perfect stocks to work with as a swing trader because they provide you with the steadiest gains. Trading in these companies can result in you making a decent amount of money, with less risk than trading in very volatile markets.

The final consideration for picking the right trades is to calculate your risks vs. your rewards. Doing this calculation will help you determine whether your trade of choice is worth it. Your choice requires a balance between risk/reward and probability. For example, playing the lottery is a perfect risk/reward scenario since you risk only $1 for millions of dollars. However, the probability of you winning the lottery is very low. When you choose your trades based on risk/reward also take into account probability. The general rule of thumb is to risk only 1-2% of your capital. For example, if you have $5,000 to trade, you may not want to risk losing more than $50-$100 on a trade with multiple shares. Another way to determine your risk is to check your risk/reward ratio. The general rule of thumb for this ratio is 1:3 or 1:2.

Here's how to calculate your risk/reward ratio: find the amount that you are okay with losing. Divide that number by the amount you think you can make on the trade. That is your risk/reward ratio. For example, if you are willing to risk $2 per share of ABC stock and the stock is currently valued at $70, then you can place your stop-loss at $68. This is your $2 risk. For your reward, you might expect the stock to increase to $80, giving you a reward of $10. Your risk/reward ratio is $2/$10 or 1:5. If this trade is worth it to you, then this is a satisfactory risk/reward ratio.

Take all of these factors into consideration when choosing your trades and you'll have no trouble with making some profit. Keep in mind that you will have losses, but you'll also have gains. Use them both to help you analyze your next steps. While in theory all of this sounds easy, it actually requires a bit more thought than just jumping into the market. This is where trading plans and analyzing charts for patterns, come in.

Chapter Seven: Understanding Chart Patterns

We've talked a little bit about charts in the previous section. We discussed where to find swings, mapping out the support and resistance and planning your entry and exit points. But we haven't yet looked at some patterns that traders seek before making their trades. Studying these patterns can help you get an idea of where to enter and exit a trade. This chapter will discuss the patterns that you can find in a chart.

Trading patterns

History tends to repeat itself. We've heard this mantra so many times and we see it play it out in our lives. For example, politically, our countries follow patterns over and over again. We fight the same wars over and over again, make the same mistakes and repeat the same arguments with other countries. In our families, it's not too difficult seeing children growing into adults who are just like their parents, repeating their parents' and grandparents' mistakes and successes in a pattern. Trading is no different and movement of stocks from 100 years ago can still be relevant today. With over 100 years of data from trades, certain patterns have emerged that have become universal indicators for trading. Just like how we all follow the same route home every day, and never deviate, it's unlikely that trades will start a pattern and then shift in an unexpected direction. For this reason, it's a good idea to study some of the various chart patterns to find good entry and exit points. These basic patterns include the head and shoulders, the cup and handle, triangles, and crosses.

Head and Shoulders

It's rare to see a pattern and know exactly what it means for the market. However, the head and shoulders pattern is one of such patterns. It's a rare one, but it usually results in a trend reversal. This means that when you see the head and shoulders pattern over the course of six months, the price is going to reverse. For example, if a stock has been trading steadily at $200 per share, seeing a head and shoulders can indicate that the stock value is going to start a new upward trend, or that it's going to start a new downward trend.

The head and shoulders pattern looks like a large mountain with two smaller mountains on either side. The point at which the two lowest points converge is the neckline.

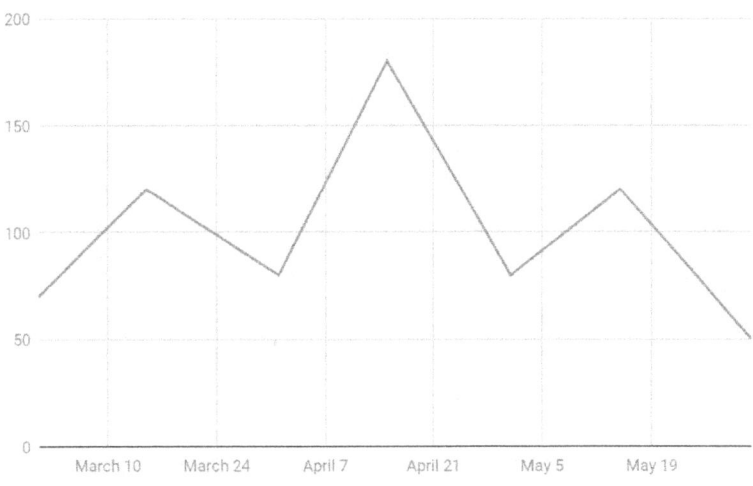

Picture 1

In this example of head and shoulders top, we can see that before March, the stock was cruising somewhere between $50 and $100, probably in an upwards trend. But then we see the head and shoulders indication, with some large swings up and down again.

We can see that it peaked once at $120 before reversing, then peaked again at $180 before reversing. Then there is a final peak that doesn't reach the highest point. In May, we can see that the stock is now taking the plunge downwards. We can make a neckline of the lowest points in the head and shoulders. This neckline is at $80. If the value drops below the neckline, it means that the pattern will play out. In this pattern, the head and shoulders indicate that a new trend will be a bearish (downturn) in prices. This example is very dramatic, but head and shoulders can occur at any price, even between a couple of dollars.

Notice how the pattern emerges over the course of several months. Many traders believe that the longer it takes to emerge, the more likely that the market will turn to follow its pattern indication. In this case, with three months of head and shoulders pattern, the stock value is very likely to drop into a downward trend.

Head and shoulders can also show the reverse, called head and shoulders bottom. It marks the beginning of a new upward trend. Here is an example.

Picture 2

In this example, we can see a reverse head and shoulders. Before March, the trend of the stock was in a downward position, coming from $75. In March the first shoulder formed. This is the first dip down to $30 before rebounding up to $80. Then it drops again forming the head at $20. It rebounds once more to $80 again, before taking its final, smaller dip. After this, the trend turns to an upward trend. The price has to move past the neckline. In this case, the neckline is sitting pretty at $80. When the price moves above that, it completes the pattern and marks the start of a new upward trend.

For a swing trader, a head and shoulders pattern can be a boom looking at the head and shoulders bottom pattern (the second chart), a swing trader could follow the pattern and enter the market right after the last shoulder. A good entry price would be $60, the stop-loss at $50, and then the trader can consider how much risk they want to take on before exiting using their risk/reward ratio. If you wanted to, you could try swing trading in the upward or downward trend of the head and shoulders, but this comes with more risk. Before seeing the pattern emerge, it would be hard to know when the reversals will come, so stick with your entry and exit plans.

Remember that these example charts are fairly extreme and prices don't often move this much. For a swing trader, you're more likely to see the head and shoulders in smaller dollar amounts. However, keeping an eye out for it could provide you with decent returns.

Cup and Handle

Most of us are aware of the shape of a tea cup. It has a slow, progressive "U" shape that extends to the handle, which drops downward. This is the image you're looking for in a cup and handle pattern: a downward "U" shaped trend that comes back up, before following the handle into a slight downturn.

A cup and handle pattern usually indicates that the market prices are going to increase. This means that finding the cup and handle can present you with buying opportunities. Here is an example of the cup and handle pattern:

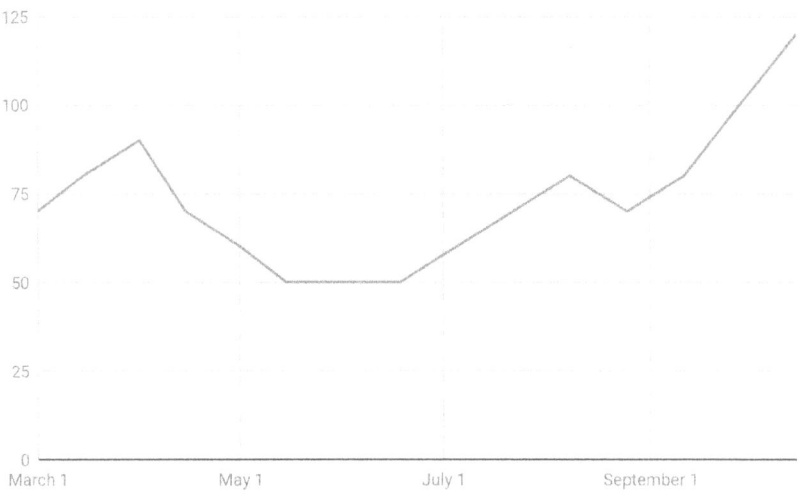

Picture 3

In the cup and handle example above, we can see the shape of the "U", the handle that comes off the right side, and then the lift-off into an upwards trend. Before May, we can see that the stock price was already at an upwards trend before it started dropping down. By June, the prices were at $50 per share. Then the prices increased to $80 per share in August. This was the end of the cup. The handle started right after with a slight decrease in price to $70 before increasing again and continuing the trend line.

As a swing trader, you can trade within the cup, by the handle, or right after the handle. This chart's line is pretty solid, but in reality, it's full of little swings up and down. You could choose to trade in those smaller swings for a few dollars of gain. Or you could trade at the bottom of what you perceive to be the cup and exit somewhere higher. This is a larger swing that would take several weeks instead of a couple of days. Your decision to trade has to be based on your risk tolerance. Wherever you choose to trade, it's a good idea to place your stop-loss at the bottom of the cup or below the handle. That way you're protected if the cup or handle descends to a level you weren't expecting.

When looking for a cup and handle pattern, make sure that you are giving it enough of a timeline. A lot of traders suggest that more time in the cup means that the indications of a bullish market afterwards are correct. So, with more time, comes more certainty. In the example above we can see that the cup and handle formation took roughly 6 months to develop and end. Because the cup and handle pattern isn't always precise, it's important to check for other indicators of a market change beyond the pattern.

Triangles

Triangle patterns can help you see how a pattern will continue and won't have any major reversals. The ascending triangle can show that the current upwards trend will continue, despite some fluctuations. Here is an example:

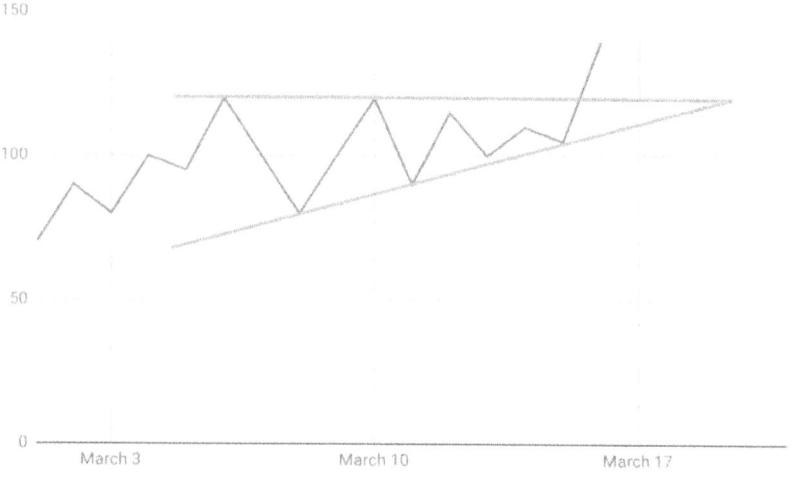

Picture 4

We can see from this example that the stock was already in an upwards trend. Then, there's some volatility. From March 7 - March 17, we can see some peaks and valleys. However, notice that the valleys remain on the trend line, and the peaks don't exceed resistance until it finally breaks out on March 15. This is an ascending triangle. It shows that the trend will continue its past pattern and remain in an upwards direction.

Depending on if you want to swing trade within the triangle, or trade once the triangle is over, you can make some considerable profit. Seeing the ascending triangle is a clear indication of which way the market will go. If you are options trading, this is the perfect time to buy call options and then sell them at a higher premium.

If you're trading the stock itself, you can enter into the trade one or two days after the break-out point, where the triangle ends and the stock rises above the current prices. You want to wait a few days to counteract any reversals back into the triangle. You can also enter right after the first valley. It's up to you. You can place a stop-loss just under the first valley point if you plan on trading in the swings of the triangle.

While the ascending triangle shows a continuous upward trend, the descending triangle shows the opposite. It shows how the current downwards trend will continue, despite some fluctuations. Here is an example:

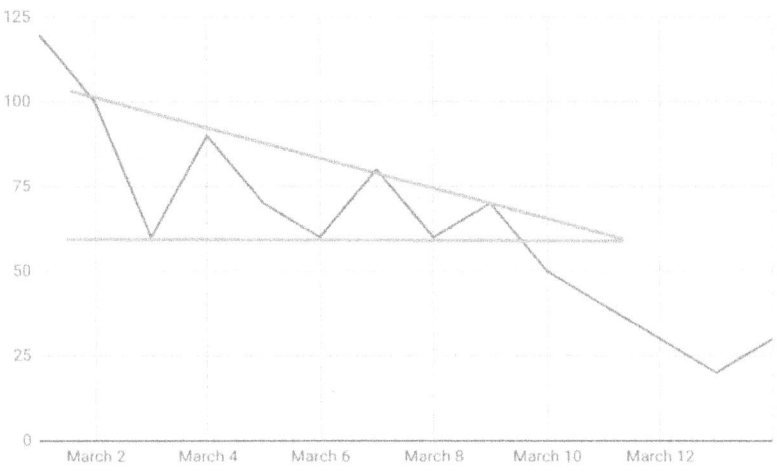

Picture 5

In this example we can see that the downward trend started before March. And while there are some signs of it trying to get back up there, the price is still dropping. Notice how the peaks on March 4th, March 7th and March 9th are all lower than the previous peaks. Also notice how the lows are consistently at the same level. The moment that the stock price breaks out of the support line, then you'll know the downward trend will continue for this stock.

For trading, this stock is a good option for swing trading as all of the swings can provide you with some profit if you time them right. This could also be an opportunity for put options, which will net you a small profit. Remember that if you choose to enter the market after the break out, you should wait a couple of days before placing your trades. This will give the trend enough time to solidify and give you enough time to make sure the trend won't give one more upswing.

Golden Cross

As cool as the golden cross sounds, it's not as awesome looking at it. Unlike head and shoulders or cup and handles, there isn't a solid visual representation in the stock value itself. Instead, the golden cross is seen with the moving average lines. Typically, on any stock website that shows charts, you'll be able to see the stocks and then turn on the choice for moving averages. There are two moving average numbers you can choose from: the short-term average and the long-term average. Generally, people choose a 50-day moving average for the short-term one and a 200-day moving average for the long-term one.

In order to see a golden cross, you have to look for a steady 200-day moving average that then gets crossed in an upwards direction by the 50-day moving average. Here's an example, courtesy of Yahoo Financial and Google's 2016 chart:

Picture 6

The purple line is the 50-day moving average and the orange line is the 200-day moving average. Notice how the 200-day moving average is going in a steady uptrend, but then the 50-day moving average cuts across twice. The second cut is a golden cross. After the golden cross, you can see how the trend continued upwards, creating a bullish market for this stock. A golden cross indicates a new, stronger direction for the stock. In this case, Google's stock increased moving from 725 up to 927 within a few months. This is a significant uptrend. The golden cross indicator was then correct in predicting that the market would go higher.

As a swing trader, you can use the golden cross to help you make profitable upswing trades. Another choice is to buy call options right after the golden cross, and sell them once the premium has increased because the underlying stock's value has increased. Whichever direction you choose, a gain is likely since the golden cross indicates a significant uptrend.

Death Cross

While the golden crosses name indicates good things to come, the death cross is obviously more negative, but it deals with the same indicators that the golden cross does. The 200-day moving average and 50-day moving averages are what you are looking for in regards of the death cross. In a death cross, you'll see the 50-day moving average cross the 200-day moving average in a downwards direction. Here's an example from Yahoo Finance and S&P 500's chart from 2018-2019:

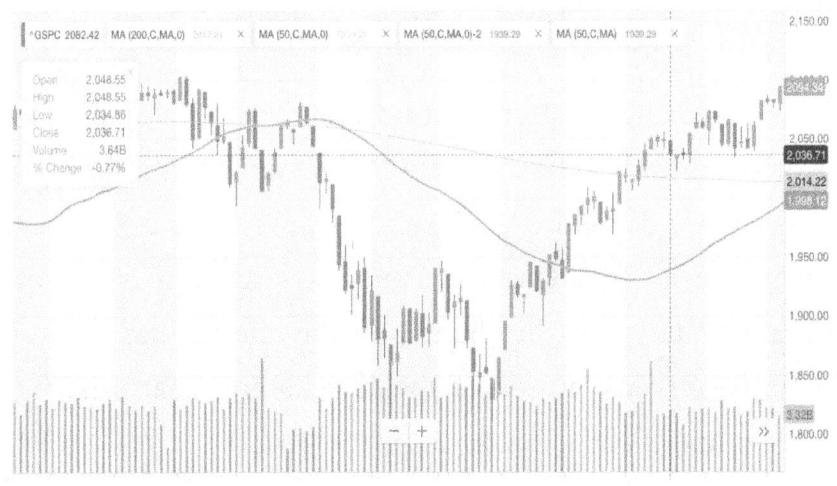

Picture 7

In this image, you can see the blue line, which indicates that 50-day moving average, crossing the orange line, the 200-day moving average. The 50-day moving average is crossing at a sharp downward angle. Where the two lines connect is the death cross. This indicates a turn in the market towards a bearish outcome. It means that there will be a significant downtrend. And, as you can see in the chart, that's exactly what happened. S&P 500's stock dropped a whopping 300 points in the course of a couple of months. Because this indicator is so clear, it's a good idea to choose your swing trades carefully. Wait a bit before purchasing or selling stock to see if the trend will reverse, but then get on with your trading.

To bring this section to a close, knowing these trading patterns can help you pick opportune times to buy into or sell a trade. There are many more trading patterns out there, so keep learning about the different kinds. Now that you know some of the basic trading patterns, it's time to practice. Search for historic charts that demonstrate these trading patterns. In this book, there's a picture of Google's charts from 2016, in that chart there is a golden cross, but there are also some other indicators that show the changes in the market. See if you can find those other indicators. To see an example chart that shows the cup and handle pattern, search for the chart of Wynn Resorts, Limited, with the tag WYNN from 2003 to 2014. You'll be able to see a very dramatic example of a cup and handle pattern. For an example of a death cross pattern, check out Facebook's stock prices (FB) in 2018. Look at the whole year and you can see multiple crosses of the 200-day and 50-day moving averages. Once you've familiarized yourself with what the patterns look like, think about how would you have traded in those charts? Also, keep your eyes open on charts that may interest you now and look for any current patterns you see emerging. Take the time to analyze what you're seeing and what choices you would make from the indications.

Chapter Eight: Making a Trading plan

Imagine wanting to design your own dream house. You're excited by all of the possibilities, so you go to the store and start picking stuff out. You don't think you need a plan because it's all in your heart and mind so you pick out some lumber that could be useful, some furnishings that might be interesting and of course, pick out the curtains. As you start building your house, you realize that the wood you bought is wrong, and because of the timing, your furnishings and curtains won't work. You go back to the store and try again and again. You see pictures of houses you like and keep adding their features to your house. Much later, your house is finally built. It's a mix of a variety of features, and it's holding itself up. It's a house that you can probably sleep in but it also cost you a lot of money, wasted materials, and time. Trading without having a plan is a lot like building a house without a plan. You can definitely make it work but it will cost you a lot of money, waste your trades, and your time.

Throughout this book, we've kept harping on the importance of having strategies and plans. That's because this is a critical skill in trading. Trading isn't about following your gut decisions. Once you start doing that, then you've gotten into random gambling instead of trading with as much precision as you can. A trading plan is vitally important and each trader should have one. It's strongly recommended that you write your trading plan down. It can be digital or physical, but having a centralized area where you can write down your trading plan, strategies and goals can help you stay on track. This can also be the area where you review your trades and keep notes for future trades. Then, before and after every trade, review your plan, add notes, and analyze your progress. To create your trading plan, start by analyzing your situation, finding your objectives and then make a trading plan.

Analyze your situation

Your trading plan should start with you understanding your situation. This goes hand in hand with the money management aspect of risk management. Understanding your situation means that you know exactly where you are financially, how much it costs to have an account for trading, and how much each trade will cost you. This means knowing which brokerage accounts you will trade out of, how much you can afford to keep in your account, how many trades you can afford in a week. All of this goes into analyzing your situation.

To find out this information, you'll have to do some research. You're already doing a great job by reading this book. But there's always more research to do. Look at the different trading firms you want to have an account in. What are their benefits or drawbacks? Do they have any incentives that might help you down the road? Make sure you know their commission costs for trades, since this comes out of your profits. Check to see if they can accommodate options trading if that's the route you're going for.

Then look into your financials and be entirely honest with yourself. How much debt do you have? Are you willing to do minimum payments on your debts and put money towards investments? Or would you rather pay more of your debt and only use a small amount for trading? It's your choice, but the point is that you need to take a good long look at your finances before getting into trading and investing. Remember, while you'll gain some from trading, you'll also likely lose some. Therefore, if you're not in the right financial situation, then wait before you begin trading capital.

Once you've understood and analyzed your situation, it's time to set out your objectives for trading.

Find your objectives

Why do you want to swing trade? This is the first question you should ask yourself when making your trading plan. It can be the first thing you write down wherever you keep your plan. This way, every time you see it and you review the plan, you're reminded of why you're doing this. Don't just leave this question unanswered. This question is the basis of all of your trades and can be the motivation to continue trading, even after a loss. Once you've analyzed your motivations, it's time to look at your goals for trading. Is your goal to save up for something, to make an income, to experiment with trading, or to have extra funds for your daily life? Knowing your overall goal can help you to then determine how much you want to make in a year of trading. Then make smaller goals moving down from the year.

All of your goals should be SMART goals. These goals are:

- **S**pecific

- **M**easurable

- **A**ttainable

- **R**ealistic

- **T**ime-bound

Specific goals are ones where you know the endpoint. A goal, for example, might be, "I want to have extra money in my account so that I can enjoy my hobby of competitive polo". Or it can be something like "I want to buy a house". While these goals are good, they're not specific enough. Try to consider things like timeline, who is helping with the goal, amount needed, and how it will be achieved. To remake the first example goal, you might say: "I want to swing trade to make $200 extra dollars to spend each month so that I can buy a horse for competitive polo by the end of the year". That is a specific goal. Now you need to determine how you will measure success towards your goal.

Measurable goals are ones that you can easily evaluate. It's basically proof that you are meeting your goal. Your measure may be seeing money in your bank account but that's pretty vague. List a specific amount you want to see each week in your account, or state what percentage you would like to make in trades. You can also see each successful trade as a measure of reaching your goal. So long as you have a clear set of numbers to assess, then you have a measurable goal because they can easily be seen and recorded. Then you'll know whether you are on track with your goal. If you're not on track, then you may need to reevaluate your process or the timeline for the goal.

Attainable goals are reachable based on how much time you have available, how much effort you put in, and the resources available to you. If your goal is to make one million dollars in a year by swing trading, you have to analyze whether or not that is attainable. Do you have the necessary funds and time to dedicate to that much trading? Do you have the knowledge that you'll need in order to make that much? Having attainable goals means that they fit into what you are capable of doing right now. If you don't have the funds, time, energy, or experience to put towards the goal, then your goal needs to be more attainable based on your current life skills and style.

Realistic goals are ones that you are actually capable of achieving. This goes hand in hand with attainable goals. Realistic goals are ones that you are capable of achieving and are relevant to you. If you know there might be a lack in an aspect of your goal, then a realistic goal includes the steps you need to take to fix it. For example, if your goal is to successfully trade by writing options, but you don't know the first thing about writing options, then this goal is not realistic. Instead, it's better to start with the goal of learning how to write options. Realistic goals need to be ones that you can honestly reach, not ones that are sky-high. Otherwise, you're just setting yourself up for disappointment.

Time-bound goals are ones that have a very specific deadline, or multiple deadlines. If you don't have a deadline for your goal, then you may not actually work towards it. It's like writing a paper for school. If your teacher says you can turn it in whenever, it's very likely it will never be turned in. But if you have a specific time that paper needs to be turned in, then you'll work hard to get it finished in time. You want to do the same with your goals. Make time goals, or specific deadlines you would like to meet to ensure that you are actually progressing. How you measure the time is up to you. A lot of people use physical graphs they can chart to show that they're meeting their timing goals. This way, it's something you have to do on paper, and something you can keep in a convenient place like your bathroom mirror, or fridge. Having a physical time tracker can be really lovely because you can see your success right there in front of you. You can also add it into your trading plan so that at the end of the goal, when you've reached it, you can go back and review your progress. Either way, having some time-bound goals will make reaching your goals easier and give you a sense of satisfaction when you make it before your deadlines.

All of these steps are what make good goals, great. However, sometimes the goal doesn't work out and it needs to be reevaluated. Reevaluating your goal is not a negative thing, it just means that you need to clarify it, find out what to change, and adapt your goal into a smarter one. When you've made your goals as clear as possible, then you're put on a road to successfully completing your goals.

Once you have chosen your goals for swing trading, it's time to get down to brass tacks and create your investment plan.

Make the trading plan

Now that you have the preliminary parts of your plan in place, it's time to really make your trading plan. In your trading plan, you need to include a lot of information regarding your investment strategies and management. This is critical because in the heat of the moment with a trade, you need to know exactly what you're doing and why. Without a trading plan, you're likely to misjudge your trades and the market, resulting in considerable loss. You'll also be more likely to trade in random areas, maybe based on your gut-feelings. However, this isn't an ideal way to trade. Take the time to figure out your strategies and put them in your trading plan. Here are some questions you should ask yourself to make the final section of your plan:

- How are you going to manage your emotions before a trade? We've already discussed the importance of managing your emotions while trading. Now's the time you make a plan for it. At what point will you know your emotions are too involved and when it's time for you to step back? How will you know if your hesitation to jump into the trade is because of poor indicators or because of fear? What should you or your family look out for in your behavior that shows it's time to take a break from trading? It's important to answer these questions. Also, talk to your loved ones about it. If you get really stressed during a trade and take out that stress on your loved ones, then they need a say in how you're managing your trade emotions too.

- How are you going to choose your stocks and options? We've talked about a lot of different factors for choosing options and stock. But what are you going to look for specifically? Will you choose stocks and options based on the company you're interested in, or will you choose them based on an industry you're interested? Knowing this aspect of your trading plan can make it easier to set up the trade in advance. Keep a list of stocks that you're interested in following in your trading plan. Then regularly check out their charts and read up on them. Don't just wing it. Do your research.

- How are you going to analyzing the markets and when? We've talked about technical analysis and fundamental analysis. To recap, technical analysis looks at trends, support and resistance, moving averages, and patterns to find out where the market will go next. Fundamental analysis looks at the corporation, the industry, and the economy, to determine where the market will go next, or where to enter the trade. Which one will you use? Just technical analysis, which is what most swing traders do, or a combination? Which indicators will help you decide where your trade is headed? Planning this out ahead of time can save you a lot of stress later on while you're trading. Also, having a consistent way of analyzing the trades can help you learn to improve and also make your trades easier.

- What are your planned entry and exit points? Will you use limit orders and stop-losses? This goes along with the previous question. Planning out what indicators you'll look for to enter and exit a trade can help you make sure that your trade goes smoothly. Using limit orders and stop-losses can also make things easier. As a reminder, a limit order is the order to sell once your stock of choice has risen to your goal level. And a stop-loss is the order to sell once your stock drops to a certain level due to a change in the markets. Knowing that everything is set up ahead of time can really ease your mind. It also gives you the chance to enjoy your weekends and nights, since you won't be able to follow the markets well then. Take the time to plan out when you'll enter a trade, and always make sure you have your exit planned ahead of time.

- What is your tolerance for risk? Know how far you're willing to go in a trade and at what point you want to stop. For every trade determine your risk/reward ratio and keep track of it in your trading plan. What risks are you willing to take? What's the reward you're hoping to get? Knowing your risk/reward before your trades can help you make good decisions. Keeping track of them in your trading plan can give you space to analyze whether your trades were worth it or not. You can use this record of risk/reward ratios to help you plan your next steps and help you better understand your own tolerance for risk.

- When will you review your results? Don't just walk away from the trade. Take the time to review it and write down every step you took. This is especially important in the beginning so that you know what worked for you and what didn't. It's also a good time to reassess your situation based on your recent trades. Think about your losses and gains and find out where you want to go next. After reviewing, the next step is evaluating.

- How will you evaluate your results and what will you do with that evaluation? This is probably the most key step. After your trade, it's time to evaluate your progress. Were you happy with your trade? If so, why, or why not? With this question, you get into the details of why a trade worked for you and was gratifying or not. What parts would you change differently next time? What are your takeaways? These two questions are all about fine-tuning your strategies and making the most out of your losses and gains. All of this evaluation is key to improving your skills as a swing trader. Take the time to do it. Maybe take some time on a weekend to review your trades for that week, or have another day that you use to evaluate your trades. Whichever day you choose, make it a consistent one so that evaluating your trades becomes a habit you always do.

- What are your strengths and weaknesses in swing trading? Finally, at the end of your trades thinking about your strengths and weaknesses. This will show you areas where you can make improvements, and from there, you'll know what to practice next.

All of these aspects are important to include in your trading plan. Keep your plan updated regularly and always, always, follow it. If you want to have a set up that you can use with each trade, you can find trading plans online. These plans often include details for individual trades and are not an overarching plan. Therefore, you still need to make one large plan if you use an individual trading plan for your trades. Many brokers also have trading plans that you can look at and review.

After evaluating a multitude of trades, if you notice your strategy isn't working, try a new one and follow the process again. Always take notes, always see where you are improving and where improvement is needed. Trading risks your hard-working dollars, therefore make sure you are using them to the best effect by having a trading plan.

Chapter Nine: Seven Strategies to Maximize Short-Term Trading

You've learned a lot so far and we're nearing the end of the book. It's important to keep some things in mind to help you make the most out of swing trading. Remember, all of these regard trading options or trading stocks. Here are seven strategies to maximize short-term trading.

1. Practice, Practice, Practice: This may not seem like a strategy, but believe me it is. Practice gives you the chance to explore the world of swing trading without the pain of losing your money. It's an excellent way to make improvements, try out trading plans and learn about the process. You can get a demo account from a variety of websites. The demo accounts will show you exactly what you're set up is, and how it responds to the market. It makes it easier to see your moves beyond viewing the chart. Take six months to trade on a demo account before doing so with actual money. Remember, as you go through with your demo count, don't think about your trades as wins and losses. Instead, think of all of them as a growth process. You're learning and improving. Having this kind of mindset can make swing trading more worthwhile and less stressful. Keep this mindset even as

you move to real trades.

2. Have a Trading Plan and Stick with it: We've covered this a lot, but it can't be said enough. Stick with your trading plan. Always. Your trading plan is what differentiates you from an amateur who's just winging-it. If you have unlimited funds and want to just wing it, then, by all means, do so. But if you're like most of us, you only have limited funds and you need to make them work for you. A trading plan is where you're going to make the best choices for your trades.

3. Pick the Right Stocks: Choosing the right stocks from the get-go is obviously important. In your trading plan you should have a list of stocks and options on those stocks that you would be interested in trading. Generally, for swing trading you want to choose a stock that gets actively traded, has good swings, and has little volatility. This means no to small technology stocks and yes to large-cap stocks.

4. Start Small: When you learn how to do something new, do you just jump right in? Probably not. The same is true with swing trading. Don't put all of your money in one trade right off the bat. You can, if you really want to, but it's not recommended. Start with really small trades. Making a profit of $1 is better than not so work with

small trades. You'll be making some steady profits and will also be getting the chance to practice your swings without too much loss. You can increase your trade numbers after having a lot of experience but always start small.

5. Learn to Swing Trade Before Considering Options: Options are so awesome because you can trade with less capital. But unless you understand how the underlying stock moves and changes, you won't have a lot of success with options. Start by learning to swing before going into options. This means practicing with stocks. You don't have to buy a lot and you don't have to swing multiple at once. But starting with stocks first gives you an idea of how the stocks will move, and how to best swing trade with them. Once you understand that, using options will be easier, especially if you're trading with the premiums, and not exercising the options.

6. Cut Your Losses Quickly: As your swing trading, if you see a sharp turn in the market, don't stick around and wait to see how it pans out. You're not a long-term trader, you're a swing trader and you only have a small area where to get profit. If you don't have a stop-loss in place, this is especially important. Waiting to see if the market will change will cost you more losses than cutting your losses and getting out. If the market changes again, you

can always buy back in.

7. Avoid system hopping at all costs: If you see that something isn't working, it's easy to want to shift quickly in a completely new direction. However, this isn't always the wisest decision. In the case of swing trading, system hopping will cost you a lot of money. System hopping is moving from swing trading, to day trading, to trend trading, to long-term investments. If you have a diversified portfolio, then, by all means, have some long-term investments. But for the most part, you want to avoid switching your system. This is because you will have to take the time to relearn each system, change your trading plans, and keep adapting. System hopping also means you're not taking the time in one system to actually make a profit. If you're experiencing a lot of losses with swing trading, then re-evaluate your trading plan and make a new strategy. But don't just hop to the next system of trading.

Extra tip: Keep $25,000 in your brokerage account. This sounds like a lot but honestly, it can help your accounts. A lot of brokerage accounts will see you as a day trader if you are making a trade every day or four times a week. If this happens, the brokerage account will stop you from making more trades if your account drops below $25,000. If you plan on trading frequently during the week, having this amount in your account is vital. That's a set amount beyond how much you actually risk in your trades.

With these seven strategies, you'll be sure to get the most out of your swing trades.

Conclusion

Thank you for taking the time to read this book on swing trading! We've covered a lot of topics and provided you with a comprehensive guide to swing trading. Swing trading is honestly one of the best ways to get into trading. It provides beginners with the chance to make small gains and small losses while learning to understand the market and the movements of stocks. Therefore, it is the perfect trading strategy to use.

When swing trading, remember to take your time to analyze the markets. Using technical analysis, you can look at the trends of your stock of choice, or check out its simple moving average. You can find patterns in charts that can show you the best times to enter or exit a trade. And by mapping out the support and resistance on a chart, you can be sure to know which swings will be most profitable for you. If you want to add to your technical analysis, do a bit of fundamental analysis. Look at the company itself and determine if they're going to do something big in a little while, or if their finances are not good. Also, look at the industry and its projection to the future. Your use of fundamental analysis can help you improve your understanding of the market and increase your chances of finding a good entry and exit point.

Regarding entry and exit: always make sure you have everything planned out ahead of time. Don't just leave your exit up to fate. Make sure that you are using stop-losses and limit orders to protect your trades. You can also use call or put options to hedge your trades and make sure that you are getting the most out of them.

If you want to use options beyond a way to hedge your trades, then they can be a really perfect vehicle for trading. Options provide you with a lot of leverage because you can purchase them for a fraction of the price of the underlying stock and still make the same profit as if you had purchased the stock itself. That means more money in your account and less risk. Buying call options can also be a great thing to trade because if you're paying close attention to the markets, you can sell the call option to another investor and make a profit from the premiums if your time it right. While writing options will give you an income, it's not recommended since the losses can be unlimited. Instead, buy call options or put options and trade them with other investors to make profits.

Always remember that with swing trading, you're only looking to make small gains. This helps to reduce your risk because if you're only putting a little on the market, then you'll only lose a little, as long as you act smartly about it, anyways. Hedge the risks associated with swing trading by diversifying your portfolio. Do a bit of long-term investing, or work with a variety of assets. A good way to diversify is to get into a mutual fund, where you'll make some money while also reducing your risks. Think about branching out across different industries, as this will also help you with diversification. Other risk management strategies include working on your mindset, controlling any addictions and understanding basic money management skills. Take the time to make sure that you are limiting your risks as much as you can.

Finally, put together your trading plan for swing trading. This isn't the type of trading where you can just wing it and hope to make a profit. Instead, having a trading plan can ensure that you are putting your money in the best position it can possibly be in. Update your trading plan regularly and always follow it.

You're now ready to start on the process of swing trading. We hope this book has helped you understand the what's and the how's of swing trading. Keep learning and practicing and you'll do great with it. Good luck!

By the same Author:

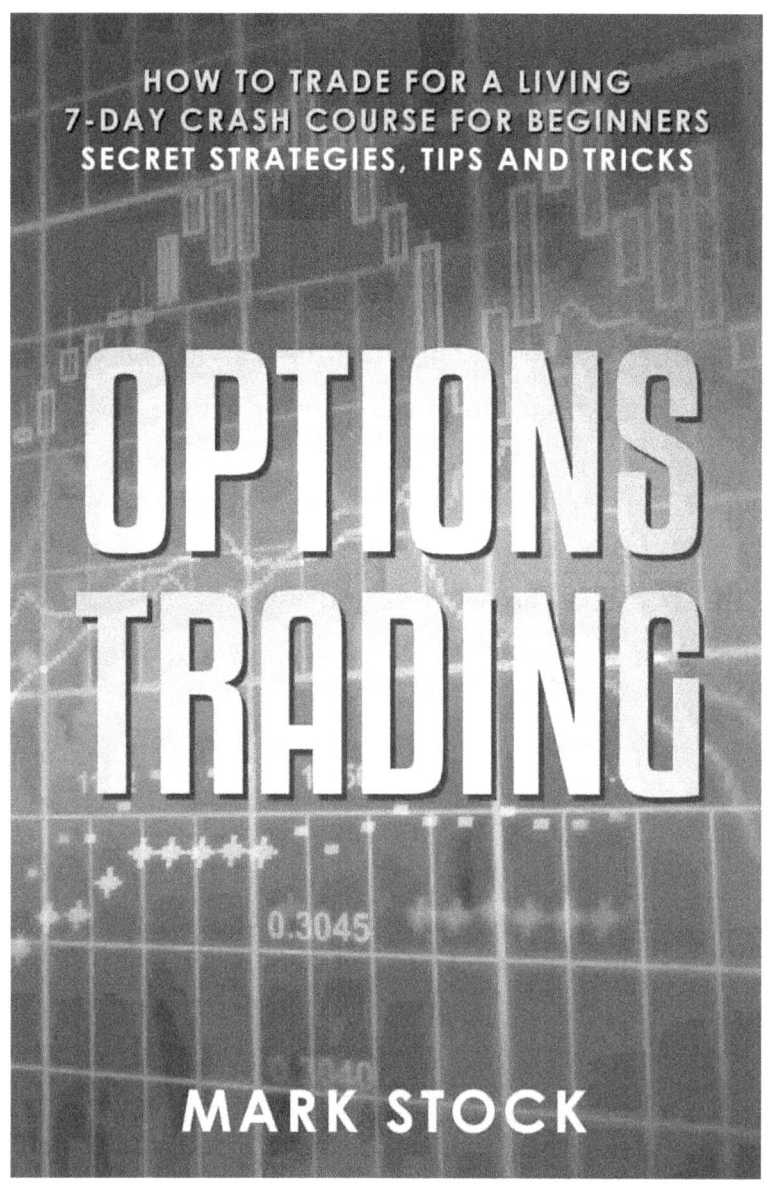

HOW TO TRADE FOR A LIVING
7-DAY CRASH COURSE FOR BEGINNERS
SECRET STRATEGIES, TIPS AND TRICKS

OPTIONS
TRADING

0.3045

MARK STOCK

CURRENCY TRADING MADE SIMPLE

THE ULTIMATE FOREX TRADING GUIDE FOR BEGINNERS

SECRET STRATEGIES, TIPS AND TRICKS

181.550 ▲ 2.47

893.094

FOREX TRADING

1.550 ▲

893.094 ▼

MARK STOCK

HOW TO SWING TRADE FROM A-Z
7-DAY CRASH COURSE FOR BEGINNERS
PROVEN STRATEGIES, MONEY MANAGEMENT AND TRADING TOOLS

SWING TRADING

MARK STOCK

SWING TRADING
FOR BEGINNERS

A COMPREHENSIVE BEGINNER'S GUIDE PROVEN STRATEGIES, MONEY MANAGEMENT AND TRADING TOOLS

MARK STOCK

OPTIONS TRADING
FOR BEGINNERS

HOW TO TRADE FOR A LIVING
7 DAY CRASH COURSE:
SECRET STRATEGIES, TIPS AND TRICKS

MARK STOCK